POWER IN SERVICE

CURRENT AND FORTHCOMING TITLES

ACADEMIC INTRODUCTIONS
FOR BEGINNERS

AVAILABLE

TO BE RELEASED IN 2014

TO BE RELEASED IN 2015

POWER IN SERVICE

AN INTRODUCTION TO
CHRISTIAN POLITICAL THOUGHT

BY

WILLEM J. OUWENEEL

PAIDEIA PRESS
2014

A Publication of the
REFORMATIONAL PUBLISHING PROJECT
www.reformationalpublishingproject.com
and
PAIDEIA PRESS,
P.O. Box 500, Jordan Station,
Ontario, Canada. L0R 1S0

©PAIDEIA PRESS 2014

ISBN 978-0-88815-229-9

Cover design and layout: Bill Muir

Printed in the United States of America

"Jesus came and said to them, 'All authority in heaven and on earth has been given to me. Go therefore and make disciples of all nations, baptizing them in the name of the Father and of the Son and of the Holy Spirit, teaching them to observe all that I have commanded you. And behold, I am with you always, to the end of the age.'"

Matthew 28:18-20

"Be subject for the Lord's sake to every human institution, whether it be to the emperor as supreme, or to governors as sent by him to punish those who do evil and to praise those who do good. For this is the will of God, that by doing good you should put to silence the ignorance of foolish people. Live as people who are free, not using your freedom as a cover-up for evil, but living as servants of God. Honor everyone. Love the brotherhood. Fear God. Honor the emperor."

1 Peter 2:13-17

TABLE OF CONTENTS

About the Author

Willem J. Ouweneel (1944) earned his Ph.D. in biology at the University of Utrecht (The Netherlands, 1970), his Ph.D. in philosophy at the Free University in Amsterdam (The Netherlands, 1986), and his Ph.D. in theology at the University of the Orange Free State in Bloemfontein (Republic of South Africa, 1993). Among many other things, he has been professor of the Philosophy of Science for the Natural Sciences at the University for Christian Higher Education in Potchefstroom (Republic of South Africa, 1990-1998), and professor of Philosophy and Systematic Theology at the Evangelical Theological Faculty in Leuven (Belgium, 1995-2014). He is a prolific writer (mainly in Dutch), and has preached in more than thirty countries. Several times he was a candidate for Dutch Christian political parties.

FOREWORD

The publisher of this book kindly invited me to write this introduction to Christian politicology, or political science. It is part of a series of introductions—not scholarly books, with many learned footnotes and extensive bibliographies, but of an accessible nature, suitable for students in the last years of high school, or the first years of college or university, as well as for the general public.

The first volume in this series is an introduction to Christian philosophy. For a proper understanding of the present introduction to politics, it is highly recommended to read this previous volume first.

In this short study, the phenomenon of the state is investigated in the context of the biblical notion of the Kingdom of God. This notion is not just of theological interest but also of great significance in many other Christian studies, not least in social studies and treatises related to the state and Christian politics.

Please note, when I use the word "state" throughout this book, I am not thinking of the fifty states that together form the United States of America, but of the nation state as a whole, in this case, the American nation state.

People who have greatly helped me through their writings or personal advice are, in alphabetical order, Dutch philosopher Dr. Herman Dooyeweerd († 1977) (especially his book *De christelijke staatsidee* ["The Christian Idea of the State"]); Australian born Dr. Stuart Fowler (especially his books *The State in the Light of the Scriptures* and *Christian Schooling*); Dutch lawyer André Rouvoet (especially his book *Reformatorische staatsvisie* ["Reformational View of the State"] (from 2007 to 2010, Rouvoet was the minister of youth and family affairs in the Dutch government); Dr. Egbert Schuurman (former senator in the Netherlands, especially his book *Reformatorische cultuurvisie* ["Reformational View of Culture"]); South African Dr. Herman J. Strauss († 1995) (especially his book *Staatsleer* ["The Science of the State"]); and Dutch theologian and philosopher, Dr. Andree Troost († 2008) (especially his book *Geen aardse macht begeren wij* ["No earthly power we desire"—a quote from the Dutch translation of a well-known Luther hymn, "A Mighty Fortress"]).

The present study is a free elaboration of a Dutch publication of mine: *Regem Habemus: Het Koninkrijk Gods en de staat* ("Regem Habemus: The Kingdom of God and the State," 1995), written for the Marnix van St. Aldegonde Foundation of the Reformatorische Politieke Federatie ("Reformational Political Federation," RPF). This was one of the Christian political parties at that time in the Netherlands, which later merged into the ChristenUnie ("Christian Union"). From 2007 to 2010, the ChristenUnie—attracting Reformed and Evangelical, and even some Roman Catholic voters—was a coalition partner in the then-current Dutch government.

Bible quotations in this book are usually from the English Standard Version (ESV). If other translations are used, this is indicated (e.g., American Standard Version [ASV], New King James Version [NKJV], New International Version [NIV]).

Willem J. Ouweneel
Zeist (The Netherlands)
Autumn 2013

CHAPTER ONE

WHAT IS THE KINGDOM OF GOD?

When, in the French city of St. Quentin, the Huguenots were besieged by the Spanish (1557), an arrow was shot from outside, over the city wall. It landed in the market square. A little note was attached to it on which was written an arrogant demand to surrender. The great leader of the Huguenots was Gaspard de Coligny, who fifteen years later was to be murdered during the so-called "Massacre of Saint Bartholomew" (1572), and whose daughter Louise married William of Orange (William the Silent), "father" of the Dutch nation. Both men are forefathers of the present Dutch king, Willem Alexander. De Coligny gave the order to send the arrow back to the enemy with a little note saying, *Regem habemus*, "We have a King!" What de Coligny apparently wanted to say was, Do not underestimate us. We have a powerful King on our side, who is the King of kings! If it is not his will, you will not be able to undertake anything against us.

The Kingdom Is Still Advancing

This reply reminds us of the word of the Lord Jesus to Pontius Pilate, which tells us much about the nature of the nation state and its relationship to the Kingdom of God: "You would have no power over me if it were not given to you from above" (John 19:11). It is the King himself who speaks here: the fettered prisoner, who stands there before the earthly authorities, the Man who, somewhat later that day, was going to be "crucified in weakness" (2 Cor. 13:4), is the King of kings and the Lord of lords (Rev. 17:14; 19:16). Even today, after so many centuries, his kingdom is still "forcefully advancing" in this world (Matt. 11:12, NIV note), not through the power of weapons, nor through the power of political actions as such, but through the Holy Spirit breaking open hearts of people. "Not by might nor by [earthly, carnal] power, but by my Spirit," says the Lord Almighty (Zech. 4:6).

It is the wind of the Spirit that blows within this Kingdom of God. It blows through lives, marriages, families, churches, even through schools, companies, and states, and brings individuals and societal relationships under the dominion of Jesus Christ. Because of the Holy Spirit, it is a Kingdom of power; as Paul says, "The kingdom is not a matter of talk [i.e., of idle words] but of power" (1 Cor. 4:20). In connection with the Kingdom, Jesus told his disciples, "You will receive power when the Holy Spirit comes on you" (Acts 1:8). God's Kingdom is a domain of power. Already during his earthly ministry, Jesus told his opponents, "If I cast out demons by the Spirit of God, surely the kingdom of God has come upon you" (Matt. 12:28 NKJV). That is, where the power of the Kingdom is manifested, there the Kingdom itself has arrived.

The testimony of de Coligny did not imply that, because *his* King was more powerful than the Spanish king, Philip II, nothing bad could happen to him. On the contrary, soon afterwards the city of St. Quentin was taken by the Spanish, and de Coligny was taken prisoner until the peace of 1559. His testimony implied rather that, whatever may happen to a Christian, he unswervingly holds on to the kingship of Christ, and to the faith certainty that no evil could ever befall him without the will of him to whom all "authorities and powers" have been submitted (1 Pet. 3:22; cf. Eph. 1:21-22). "Are not two sparrows sold for a penny? Yet not one of them will fall to the ground outside your Father's care [or, knowledge]" (Matt. 10:29). Believers can often be just as "weak" as their crucified King but their final triumph is just as sure as that of the King himself. It is under *their* feet that, in the end, the God of peace will crush Satan (Rom. 16:20).

The Two Kingdoms

It is my conviction that the notion of "Christian politics"—whatever that may be, that remains to been seen—cannot be separated from the notion of the Kingdom of God. This Kingdom is, first of all, very simply God's general government over all created things, from the foundation of the world until eternity (cf., e.g.,

Exod. 15:18, "The LORD reigns [or, is King] for ever and ever"). Secondly, and more specifically, it is the manifestation of God's counsel to put this kingdom under the feet of Man, and entrust world dominion to his care (Gen. 1:28, "fill the earth and subdue it. Rule over . . . every living creature"). The first Man, the "first Adam" (cf. 1 Cor. 15:45), has utterly failed in this, for through his fall into sin Adam surrendered his rule to the power of sin, death, and Satan (Gen. 3). This is an aspect of the fall that is not often underscored but which is of great importance.

Indeed, Satan could truly say to Jesus that all the authority and splendor of the kingdoms of this world had been "given" to him (Luke 4:5-6)—and Jesus did not deny it. On the contrary, at another occasion, he recognized that there is something in this world that can be called the "kingdom" of Satan (Matt. 12:26). Three times Jesus called Satan "the prince [or, ruler] of this world" (John 12:31; 14:30; 16:11). But he could also say that, through his coming into this world and his manifestation of the power of God, apparently the Kingdom of God had arrived (Matt. 12:28). Satan, since Calvary a sentenced rebel, will never be able to compete with this Kingdom, no matter how much noise he is still making, "prowling around like a roaring lion" (1 Pet. 5:8).

What the "first Adam" has ruined, the "last Adam" is going to restore (cf. 1 Cor. 15:45-47; then vv. 24-28). In his hands is the "restoration of all things" (Acts 3:31 NKJV). If we look at Psalm 8 in the light of Hebrews 2, this transition from the first to the second Adam is beautifully brought to light. The Son of Man, under whose feet all created things are put, is no longer (the first) Adam, but "we do see Jesus, who was made lower than the angels for a little while, now crowned with glory and honor because he suffered death, so that by the grace of God he might taste death for everyone" (v. 9).

In the Old Testament, the coming of the Kingdom of God in this new, Messianic form is announced many times. A beautiful example is Isaiah 9:6-7, "For to us a child is born, to us a son is given, and the government will be on his shoulders. And he will be called Wonderful Counselor, Mighty God, Everlasting Father, Prince of Peace. Of the greatness of his government and peace there will be no end. He will reign on David's throne and over his kingdom, establishing and upholding it with justice and righteousness from that time on and forever."

Both John the Baptist and Jesus himself could say in their day that now the Kingdom of God had come "near" (Matt. 3:2; 4:17). In the person of the King, the Kingdom of God itself had arrived. As Jesus told his opponents, "Do not say, 'Here it is,' or 'There it is,' because the kingdom of God is *in your midst*" (Luke 17:21), namely, in his person. The natural-born Jew could not enter that Kingdom just like that: he had to be born again—born "of water and the Spirit"—just like any Gentile who wishes to enter the Kingdom of God. Without this "new birth," one would not even be able to "see" (grasp, understand) the Kingdom of God (John 3:1-6). Therefore, the "mysteries" of the Kingdom are only for the true disciples of the King, who keep his royal laws (see Matt. 13:22; 28:19-20). At the same time, the parables in Matthew 13 make clear that, as long as the King has not returned, the Kingdom in its outward form contains both true and false disciples (cf. also Matt. 25:14-30).

The Kingdom as Jesus Christ announced it is "not of this world" (John 18:36). This does not mean that it is not established here on earth. On the contrary. It means that it does not fit into the sinful, demonic, violent categories of "this world." The phrase "this world" refers, then, to those categories. The Kingdom of Jesus Christ is established as the very opposite of these evil powers, and until the return of the King it exists in the midst of, and over against, these evil powers. For his followers this may involve shame and persecution. Therefore, until the public coming of the King, the Kingdom largely exists in a hidden form because the King himself is still "hidden" (cf. Col. 3:3); he "went to a distant country" (Luke 19:12). The earth has not yet been filled with "justice and righteousness" (cf. Isa. 9:7), or with the "knowledge of the glory of the Lord" (Hab. 2:14), and this will not, and cannot, take place as long as the King has not re-appeared.

On the other hand, the Kingdom of God is clearly visible. You can perceive it *everywhere* where you find people who have submitted their lives to the dominion of the Lord Jesus Christ, not only their individual lives but also their marriages, their families, their churches, their schools, their companies, their societies, and even their states (if they have a good majority in them). In this way, Jesus' followers form a kind of bridgehead for the King in this world, until he will come to utterly defeat his enemies.

The last thing the "world" has seen of the King is that he was laid in a tomb. But his disciples know his "secret": they know of his resurrection and glorification, they know that all things have been put under his feet, and that "all authority in heaven and on earth" has been given to him (Matt. 28:18). Behind the stage, Jesus Christ has the reins in his hands. His disciples know this; therefore, they love him, they serve him, and they follow him with joy. Indeed, the Kingdom is a realm of love: God "has delivered us from the power of darkness and conveyed us into the kingdom of the Son of His love" (Col. 1:13 NKJV).

The Dominion of Christ

We have found two things that are both true: the Kingdom is "hidden" because the King is still "hidden." But the Kingdom is also manifest in that it comes to light at all places where the rule of Christ and his commandments are being recognized in individual hearts and lives, as well as in the societal relationships or communities, insofar as Christians can make their mark on them. I will give you a few examples.

A Christian family is part of the Kingdom of God, not necessarily because all the children have already committed their hearts and lives to the King, but because the parents have brought the family under the dominion of Christ. "In this family we recognize Jesus Christ as our King and Lord," is the confession of these believing parents.

A Christian school is part of the Kingdom of God, not necessarily because all the pupils have already committed their hearts and lives to the King, but because the administrators and the teachers have brought the school under the dominion of Christ. They tell the pupils, as it were, "At this school we maintain—in all weakness—the rules of the King, we teach you the rules of the King, and try to follow these rules ourselves." Within the safe boundaries of such a school the pupils are not "in the world," but in the wonderful realm of Christ, that is, the Kingdom of God.

A Christian company is part of the Kingdom of God, not necessarily because all its employees have committed their hearts and lives to the King, but because the employers have brought the company under the dominion of Christ. They tell the employees, "In this company, we endeavor to maintain Christian principles of justice and fairness." This is nothing else but telling the employees that they, the employers, want this company to be part of the Kingdom of God.

A Christian state—perhaps the Dutch Republic of the seventeenth century was a fair approximation of it—respects the various views and liberties of all its citizens, but is nevertheless part of the Kingdom of God. This is not necessarily because all its citizens are Christians, but because the authorities introduce and maintain Christian principles into this state, as this comes to light in their way of ruling, and in legislation that is in accordance with the Scriptures.

Separation of Church and State

Let me tell you right away that the things I have just described have nothing to do whatsoever with the notion of the separation of church and state. There is a tremendous misunderstanding here. The separation of church and state is a great thing, for which we can all be very thankful. We know from the past what it means when the church rules over the state. This is what the Roman Catholic Church did in the Middle Ages, for instance, by condemning heretics, and then handing them over to the state authorities to be executed. We also know what it means when the state rules over the church, and tells her what to believe and what not to believe, as in communist countries (e.g., North Korea).

Later on I will explain in more detail that church and state— and each family, each school, each company, each association, etc.—is to be sovereign within its own sphere of influence. Churches should not meddle in state affairs (and family affairs), and states should not meddle in the affairs of churches, families, schools, etc.

Now the tremendous misunderstanding is this: *the separation of church and state has been turned into a separation between religion and society.* I do not know whether this happens on purpose, or unconsciously, but it is quite a malicious confusion that is introduced here. Since the time of the Enlightenment (eighteenth century), spiritual and political leaders have tried, ever more openly and actively, to ban religion entirely from the public domain. This is what we call *secularization*: religion has been pushed back to the edge of society, that is, to the private lives of individual people. This is a great triumph for the kingdom of Satan, I must say, and a great drawback for the Kingdom of God. We are all guilty of this, for we have all let it happen. We ourselves have sometimes accepted this confusion between the separation of church and state, on the one hand, and the separation between religion and society, on the other. We ourselves have sometimes begun to believe that religion is a strictly private matter, and that society and the state are (supposed to be) neutral.

Listen: I do not wish for a moment that *any church denomination should control the state*. I would move abroad if that would happen in my own country. But at the same time, I maintain that the neutral state does not exist. It is nonsense. Within the boundaries of the nation state, the battle between the kingdom of Satan and the Kingdom of God is raging all the time. The same happens within so many families, schools, companies, and—unfortunately—even church denominations and local congregations. But in the state it is perhaps most conspicuous. As long as the King has not yet returned, we cannot escape from this battle. But at least we can do our best to bring to light the Kingdom of God within our own families, and within the schools we send our children to, and within the companies we found, and within the associations, societies, unions, and clubs we form.

Do not worry: we make sure to keep "church and state" carefully apart. But at the same time, we recognize that "all of life is religion," that is, all of life is under the dominion of sin and Satan or under the dominion of Christ (or, as unfortunately is often the case, a bit under both). We do not want any *church* to rule our states, families, schools, and companies, but we definitely want *Christ* to rule our states, families, schools, and companies. *All things* have been put under his feet (Eph. 1:22; Heb. 2:8)—that includes all the societal relationships and communities we are involved in. What God already did objectively, we want to do ourselves subjectively as an act of faith and love: place all our societal relationships under the feet of Christ. *We do not believe in the illusion of neutrality.* A battle is going on, especially a battle over our children, in which no individual and no institution can pretend to be neutral. An enemy who overtly presents himself as an enemy is to be preferred to an enemy presenting himself as neutral. We prefer the "roaring lion" (1 Pet. 5:8) to the "angel of light" (2 Cor. 11:14). The former wears wooden shoes, as we would say in Dutch—the latter wears slippers.

It is unthinkable that the Kingdom of God, as some would have it, encompasses only a few domains of life: your private life, your family, and your church. That would be it. If this were true, it would mean that our schools, our companies, our associations, have to be delivered up to the kingdom of Satan. We cannot let that happen. It is unbiblical and irresponsible. The Kingdom of God manifests itself in *all domains of life*. This comes to light in that officials in these domains—parents, elders, bishops, teachers, professors, employers, administrators, authorities, etc.—wield their authority in the concrete, explicit recognition that they themselves stand under the authority and commandments of Christ the Lord. This implies that those who are under these officials—children, church members, pupils, students, employees, citizens, etc.—recognize and obey this authority as the authority of the King himself.

In brief: all Christians are to behave as disciples of the King, who live, work and serve out of a burning love for him, whether it is in their marriages, their families, their churches, their schools, their companies, their associations, their political parties, and in their nation states.

Christ and the Gods

Of course, the ultimate destruction of the evil powers will also definitely involve the end of all apostate states. In Psalm 110, which Jesus quotes to the Pharisees and relates to himself (Matt. 22:41-46), it is said of the Messiah, "he will crush kings on the day of his wrath" (v. 5b). Jesus is the "ruler of the kings of the earth" (Rev. 1:5). And already now, the message comes to all heads of state, and all government leaders in this world, "I have installed my king on Zion, my holy mountain. . . . Therefore, you kings, be wise; be warned, you rulers of the earth. Serve the Lord with fear and celebrate his rule with trembling" (Ps. 2:6, 10). This is why we make intercession "for kings and all those in authority," not only in order that "we may live peaceful and quiet lives"—it is the task of authorities to take care of that—but because "God our Savior wants all people to be saved and to come to a knowledge of the truth" (1 Tim. 2:1-4).

"May all kings bow down to him and all nations serve him" (Ps. 72:11). Every "king" in this world, every head of state, every president, every prime minister, will one day bow down before Christ. Either he or she does it voluntarily already in the present age—or he or she will do it forcibly before the judgment seat of Christ. "God exalted him to the highest place and gave him the name that is above every name, that at the name of Jesus every knee should bow, in heaven and on earth and under the earth, and every tongue acknowledge that Jesus Christ is Lord, to the glory of God the Father" (Phil. 2:9-11).

At the beginning of this section I made a connection between the evil spiritual powers and nation states (or state leaders). This requires some clarification. In the New Testament, Satan, the great apostate "angelic prince," is called the "god of this age" (2 Cor. 4:4). According to Scripture, (certain) earthly states and empires each have their own invisible "angelic prince" (see Dan. 10:13, 20-21). These are the "gods," who lead the history of their respective nations, just like the Lord guides the history of his people. Clear examples of this guidance by the foreign "gods" can be found in Numbers 21:29 ("Woe to you, Moab! You are destroyed, people of Chemosh [i.e., the 'god' of Moab]! He has given up his sons as fugitives and his daughters as captives to Sihon king of the Amorites") and Judges 11:24 ("Will you not take what your god Chemosh gives you? Likewise, whatever the Lord our God has given us, we will possess") (cf. Ps. 58:1; 89:5-7).

Just like Satan himself, these "gods" are only "pretenders," "usurpers," "sentenced rebels" (Stuart Fowler). In Psalm 82, we see how God renders judgment among these alleged "gods" (notice the quotation marks in the NIV). The God of Israel is the "God of gods" (Ps. 136:2), the one "to be feared above all gods" (96:4; cf. 95:3; 97:7, 9; 135:5); among the "gods" there is none like him (86:8; 89:6).

In addition to the name "gods"—that is, celestial, created, angelic beings (cf. Ps. 29:1; Job 1 and 2, "sons of God")—there are several other names for these beings: rulers, authorities, powers, dominions, thrones (Rom. 8:38-39; 1 Cor. 2:6; Eph. 1:21; 3:10; Col. 1:16; 1 Pet. 3:22). In the great majority of the New Testament Scriptures in which these terms occur, it is immediately clear that the latter refer to angelic powers, whether good or evil. Therefore, several expositors have assumed that this is the case in *all* relevant Scriptures. This would even include Romans 13:1-7 ("Let every soul be subject to the governing authorities") and Titus 3:1 ("be subject to rulers and authorities"). These verses definitely include earthly rulers and authorities, but the underlying thought might be that these earthly authorities are led by angelic powers, whether good or evil. Also in the case of earthly rulers, we would be dealing not so much with "flesh and blood," but rather with the spiritual authorities concealed behind them (cf. Eph. 6:12).

This holds for the expression "rulers of this age," too (1 Cor. 2:6-8). Primarily, these are the men who have made themselves responsible for the crucifixion of Christ: Pilate, Herod, and Caiaphas. But the verse might be referring not only to them, but also to the spiritual powers *behind* these men, the (invisible) "powers of this dark world," the "spiritual forces of evil in the heavenly realms" (see again Eph. 6:12).

Earthly kings were often worshipped as "gods" because of their close relationship with the angelic princes "behind" them, who were the actual rulers. Thus, in Isaiah 14, behind the earthly king of Babylon, we see the image of his angelic prince ("Lucifer") looming; we find the same with the king of Tyre in Ezekiel 28. Already the church fathers often saw Satan in these angelic princes. This is not very accurate; the references are to the "gods" of Babylon and Tyre. But obviously these do relate immediately to the "god of this world," Satan. In Revelation 12, 13, 17, and 19, the "dragon," that is Satan (12:9; 20:2), is *the* angelic prince of the Roman empire, which in that Bible book stands for the eschatological world power.

This is the power that in the end will be destroyed by Christ. The last battle is between the dragon and the Lamb—an extraordinary picture, especially when we see that the winner is not a fire-breathing dragon, but a fire-breathing Lamb (cf. 2 Thess. 2:8; also see Isa. 11:4).

In Summary

Already today, Jesus Christ is in charge. He is the Lord of all. The recognition of this, which is possible only through the Holy Spirit (1 Cor. 12:3), is a condition of salvation: "If you declare with your mouth, 'Jesus is Lord,' and believe in your heart that God raised him from the dead, you will be saved" (Rom. 10:9).

Jesus has been elevated above all "authorities and powers," above all the "gods" of this world, and consequently above all earthly authorities. By whatever spiritual powers the earthly authorities may be governed, Christ has the supremacy over both the earthly authorities and the spiritual powers behind them. If these earthly authorities consider themselves to be neutral, they are utterly mistaken. There *are* no neutral families, no neutral schools, no neutral companies, and certainly no neutral states. On the one hand, they may be tools in the hands of the evil spiritual powers. On the other hand, even the most wicked governments are "God's servants" (Rom. 13:4), because he is the "God of gods."

"The king's heart is in the hand of the Lord like the rivers of water; he turns it wherever he wishes" (Prov. 21:1, cf. nkjv). This biblical fact does not take away anything from the authorities' own responsibility. But at least it shows that, behind the stage, the Lord is in charge, and that surely the claim is as false as it can be that states, or schools, could ever be neutral institutions. That is just an illusion of Enlightenment humanism.

Questions for Review

1. Describe or define "the Kingdom of God" in one sentence.

2. According to the Bible, what are the "two kingdoms"?

3. What do we mean when we say both that the Kingdom of God is "hidden," and that it is "manifest"?

4. Explain the difference(s) between the "separation of church and state" and the "separation between religion and society."

5. With respect to living in the world, every human being is under the dominion of someone or something. Do you agree or disagree? Please illustrate your answer.

6. What is "the illusion of neutrality"?

7. Explain the Bible's teaching about the spiritual powers behind earthly rulers. Where does the Bible teach the existence of angels and of a "world of angels"?

Chapter Two

CHURCH AND STATE APART

In the first volume of the present series of introductory books, *Wisdom For Thinkers*, I have tried to explain a very important principle. This was developed by Abraham Kuyper (1837-1920), who was a Dutch pastor, theologian, journalist, and politician. An extraordinary man! He founded both a new church denomination and a new university, and he was even prime minister of the Netherlands from 1901 to 1905. The principle Kuyper developed is that of so-called *sphere sovereignty* (in Dutch, "soevereiniteit in eigen kring"). Basically, he wanted to express by this principle that neither the church should rule over the state, nor the state over the church, but that each is relatively sovereign within its own sphere or domain of activity.

Kuyper's message was: Do not interfere with each other's sphere! The state has the responsibility of maintaining *public justice* (I will explain this term later in this chapter), and thus has to create the outward conditions under which churches can operate. But the state does not meddle in the internal affairs of churches. The same holds for marriages, families, schools, associations, political parties, etc.: each is sovereign within its own sphere, without interference either from the state, or from the church. Even a Roman Catholic or a Reformed school is not to be run by Roman Catholic or Reformed church leaders *as such*, but by Roman Catholic or Reformed *school leaders*.

Sphere Sovereignty

Let us now look a bit more closely at this notion of sphere sovereignty. For instance, the state as such has nothing to say about what goes on in people's bedrooms, or how parents educate their children, about how schools teach pupils, about what people companies will do business with, about whether women are to be allowed in pulpits, etc. But the state does maintain public justice, so it does have something to say about husbands raping their wives, about parents or teachers abusing the children entrusted to them, about education in schools in terms of academic quality, about companies that operate illegally, about churches having loud praise meetings in the middle of the night, etc.

Shortly after the Reformation, this relative power of the various spheres, especially that of the nation state, was not yet clearly discerned. In England, the king, as head of state, also became the head of the Church of England, and as such ordered a new Bible translation, which became known as the *King James Bible*. In the Netherlands, it was not the Reformed church but the States-General that convened the famous international Synod of Dort (1618-1619), and also ordered a new Bible translation, the *Statenvertaling* (the States-General translation). Today, such dominance of the state over church life would be unthinkable in any civilized country.

In the worst case scenario, a state ruling over its citizens' private lives, their marriages, their churches, the way they educate children, a state that in fact owns all the schools and all the companies, is a dictatorial, and often even terrorizing, system. It is totally against the Christian notion of the state as a strictly juridical system. In the Christian view, the state creates the necessary legal preconditions for an optimal functioning of societal life, but at the same time guarantees the freedom and unique responsibility of its citizens, individually as well as in their churches, schools, companies, associations, etc.

The state can easily go wrong here. Socialism has ideological reasons for giving too much authority to the state, that is, for giving it too many responsibilities that actually belong to the citizens. Classic liberalism (the foundation of libertarianism) does the opposite: it has ideological reasons for minimizing the state's authority, so that the state cares too little about those citizens who are hardly able to stand on their own feet (the weak, the sick, the aged, the disabled, etc.), or who have no other people to help them. In a Christian view of the state, both ideological pathways, commonly identified today as socialism and libertarianism, are fundamentally rejected. In such a Christian view of politics, the power of the state concerns only "public justice" (see below), but this does include looking after the weak, as we will see later.

Also when it comes to the church's sphere of influence and authority, it is important to emphasize the meaning of sphere sovereignty. I said that the state should not rule over the church, but the opposite is also true: the church should not rule over the state. As I said before, that was the case in medieval Roman Catholic Europe, where the church could condemn someone for (alleged) heresy, and then hand him over to the state to receive the death penalty. Today, that would be unthinkable in any civilized country. Actually, the situation in Iran is largely like this. Here, the spiritual leaders, the *ayatollahs*, hold the real political power, and the president is subservient to them.

Other Societal Relationships

The notion of sphere sovereignty does not involve only churches and states. The whole question of the separation of church and state has laid too much emphasis on just these two institutions. In historical cases in which the state ruled over the church (I mentioned England and the Netherlands), the state was usually considered to be a "Christian" state (just like Iran, where the *ayatollahs* are in charge, is a Muslim state). In such a situation, no one considers either the state or the church to be neutral. But what about all the other societal relationships or communities, such as families, schools, and companies? Could these ever be religiously neutral?

Here I have to emphasize again that there are no neutral people, or neutral societal relationships. The state ought not to be under the authority of any church. But that does not alter the fact that people who exercise the state's authority are always *religious* people—in the broadest sense of the term, which includes even political ideologies and atheism—whether they like it or not. That is, they stand before God as his servants (Rom. 13), whether they like it or not. They will have to give an account to him. The church does not have the monopoly on religion! *All* people are religious in the sense of being oriented toward some Ultimate Ground of certainty and confidence, whether this is God or particular idols. Therefore, not only churches but also states, schools, companies, associations, etc. are responsible to God, and have to give an account to him.

In fact, in the United States, the two major parties, Republican and Democrat, have always implicitly recognized that politics is not religiously neutral. How else could we explain that, traditionally, Northeastern Protestants for the great majority have historically voted Republican, whereas Roman Catholics, Jews, African-Americans, and Southern Protestants for the great majority have historically voted Democrat? The reason why this is so is a fascinating subject in its own right; the discussion of it would carry us too far afield. Suffice it to say that religion obviously plays a role in American politics as can be seen in the political choices people make, even if the Republican and Democrat parties are not explicitly Christian parties.

By the way, not every Christian thinker is very keen on the term "sphere sovereignty" as such. Some people prefer to speak of the distinct "offices and responsibilities" of, and within, the various societal relationships (families, churches, states, schools, companies, parties), while others like to speak of "structural pluralism." Personally, I do not like any "-ism"; I would rather speak of a social-structural "plurality." But what's in a name? The point that matters right now is the insight that society consists of a number of distinct relationships or communities, each of which is rooted in a divine order (I have explained this in *Wisdom for Thinkers,* see chapter 4), and in which every human has his or her own task and responsibility. These societal relationships are mutually irreducible and do not stand in some hierarchical order, so that none of them is allowed to rule over the others, neither the state, nor the church. Each societal relationship or community stands directly under God's sovereign rule.

The Kingdom and God's Righteousness

In order to explain the various aspects of this important subject in more detail, I believe that the following notions need to be dealt with: (a) the notion of *public justice,* as a fundamental principle in

Christian politics (sometimes referred to as the "common good"), (b) the notion of *theocracy*, one of the most misunderstood principles in Christian politics, (c) the notion of the Christians being *exiles and pilgrims* in this world (Eph. 2:19; cf. 1 Pet. 1:1), and (d) the Lutheran notion of the *two regiments*. This will be our agenda for chapters 3-5 in this book.

Public justice is a facet of biblical justice or righteousness, which is a vital element within the Kingdom of God. When the Lord Jesus says, "Seek first his [i.e., God's] kingdom and his righteousness" (Matt. 6:33), he is apparently referring to righteousness, both public and private justice, as a matter that touches the essence of God's Kingdom. It is said of the Messiah, "See, a king will reign in righteousness and rulers will rule with justice" (Isa. 32:1; cf. 9:7; 11:4-5). These terms, *righteousness* and *justice*, do not refer only to the future new heavens and new earth, although it is said that righteousness will dwell there (2 Pet. 3:13). If it were only a notion for the future, how then could the Christian be called to pursue God's Kingdom and his righteousness—public or private—already today? Sure, there is a big difference: in the end, righteousness will rule when all *un*righteousness will have been taken away and all powers of *un*righteousness will have been destroyed. Today, we seek righteousness in the midst of, and over against, a world full of unrighteousness; this is the pursuing of unrighteousness that Solomon (Prov. 15:9), Isaiah (Isa. 51:1), and Paul (1 Tim. 6:11; 2 Tim. 2:22) speak about.

When Paul refers in Romans 14:17 to the Kingdom of God, he definitely speaks of it as a present reality, and yet as a Kingdom that is "a matter of . . . righteousness and peace and joy in the Holy Spirit." He says this in spite of all the *un*righteousness, all the disharmony and disorder, all the battles and conflicts, and all the sadness and emptiness still around us. In the midst of all this, Paul maintains, there is a realm of righteousness, peace, and joy in the Holy Spirit. And when Jesus speaks about the Kingdom in *his* day, he sees it as an empire that is "forcefully advancing" (Matt. 11:12 NIV note), that is, a Kingdom that is introducing God's righteousness into this world, over against all the "violent people raiding it," all powers of *un*righteousness that want to stop and overwhelm this Kingdom.

17

Of course, no nation state is identical with the Kingdom of God, for this Kingdom involves a kind of righteousness that reaches much farther than just the domain of public justice. The Kingdom of God "forcefully advances" in civic life wherever and whenever authorities and citizens bow before God's Word. It does so even when only some of the authorities and citizens respect God's Word. In doing so, they still put the mark of God's King- dom—no matter how imperfectly—on the functioning of the state. Likewise, the Kingdom of God "forcefully advances" in marriag- es and families, wherever and whenever husband and wife, par- ents and children, bow before God's Word. Even if only one of the marriage partners bows before God's Word, this one person puts the mark of God's Kingdom on that marriage and that entire fam- ily. This is, I presume, the sense of 1 Corinthians 7:14, where Paul argues that the believing wife places the stamp of God's Word on her marriage or family in such a way that her husband and chil- dren are "sanctified" and "holy," respectively. Even if they would still have an unregenerate heart, they do find themselves in the hallowed atmosphere of the Kingdom of God, where God's Word reverberates and the Holy Spirit is working.

Even the pseudo-Christians, who eventually "fall away," have for a time "shared in the Holy Spirit" (Heb. 6:4; they have been "partakers of the Holy Spirit," ASV). This does not necessarily im- ply that the Holy Spirit has *dwelt* in these people—this is the case only in true believers (1 Cor. 6:19)—but that they have been in the atmosphere of the Kingdom of God, that blessed domain where God's Word is preached and his Spirit is working. We often find it hard to imagine what the free preaching of God's Word can do in a society. It is no wonder that Satan tries to push religion to the very edge of society (secularization)—he knows the power of that Word and that Spirit! In their spiritual battle, believers use "the sword of the Spirit, which is the word of God" (Eph. 6:17).

In a similar way, the Kingdom of God is "forcefully advanc- ing" in schools and companies, associations and parties, wher- ever God's Word, the measuring-rod of God's righteousness, is maintained and observed, no matter how weakly. Perhaps only a few of the teachers, or the employers, or the administrators in such societal relationships, manifest themselves as followers and servants of the King. However, through their testimony and their obedience to the Word of God and the dominion of Christ—in education, management, and administration—they should be able to have an impact on such societal relationships or communities as a whole. In spite of all the opposing forces of Satan and sin, in such relationships something would become visible of the Kingdom of God "forcefully advancing."

That is why we need Christian schools, Christian companies, and Christian-political structures, which reject the illusion of neutrality, and maintain the righteousness, peace, and joy of God's Kingdom in their respective domains. What a mistake to seek or pursue God's Kingdom and his righteousness only in your private life, and at best in your family and in your church, but not in society, not in your schools and companies, not in your associations and political parties. What a catastrophe it would be if we, in this way, would leave the whole of public life to the evil powers. What a tragedy if the misunderstood separation of church and state, and the lie of the "privacy of religion," would lead you to such an attitude!

The State and Its Righteousness

In my book, *Wisdom For Thinkers*, (see chapter 4), I have explained extensively that all "things," including all societal relationships, function in *all* modal aspects of cosmic reality, but are *qualified*—that is, their "quality" (their being-thus-and-so) is expressed—by just a few modal aspects. Thus, all societal relationships have a juridical aspect, but generally this is not the *qualifying* aspect of any societal relationship, except the state. Marriage has a juridical aspect in that weddings are conducted according to the existing legislation in a civilized country; only that may be called a marriage that is recognized by the state as a marriage. However, marriage is not *qualified* by this juridical aspect but by the ethical aspect of mutual matrimonial love. In other words, marriage is not primarily a juridical but a loving relationship. This love aspect characterizes all other aspects, including the juridical aspect.

The family, too, has a juridical aspect, for it is said, "Children, obey your parents in the Lord, for this is *right*" (Eph. 6:1). Moreover, there is legislation that defines what families are, who belong to them, and what, for instance, the position of stepchildren and adopted children is in families. However, the family is not *qualified* by this juridical aspect but by the ethical aspect of the love between parents and children. In other words, the family, too, is not primarily a juridical but a loving community. Here too, this love aspect marks all other aspects, including the juridical aspect.

A church denomination, or a local church congregation, has a juridical aspect as well. This comes to light, for instance, in church discipline (1 Cor. 5), which is a matter of right and wrong (also cf. 1 Cor. 6:1-8). Here again, there is legislation determining what church denominations are, and what are their rights and duties. However, a church denomination, or a local church congregation, is not *qualified* by this juridical aspect. It is obviously qualified by the pistical aspect. That is, it is not primarily a juridical but a faith relationship. This faith aspect marks all other aspects, including the juridical aspect.

The state, too, has a juridical aspect; but this aspect is at the same time what qualifies, or characterizes, the state as a societal relationship or community. I remind you again of the important fact that *all* societal relationships, including the state, function in *all* modal aspects. But in the case of the state, the juridical aspect stands out. The state is primarily a juridical relationship. *In concreto* this means that—in simple terms—just as love governs a marriage, and faith governs a church, justice governs the state. All political acts have to be viewed from this juridical point of view. For instance, the state guarantees religious freedom, not because the state as such is a religious entity, but because of the principle of public justice. That is, it is just and righteous (positively) to secure for all its citizens the liberty and possibilities to live their faith individually and collectively, and (negatively) to do this in such a way that other citizens are not disturbed or harmed by it.

Similarly, the state takes care of the weak. This, too, is a matter of public justice because every citizen could come to occupy the position of the weak in such a way that he or she cannot count (anymore) on (sufficient) help from his or her community. Similarly, the state takes care of the infrastructure within its territory, such as road and waterway construction, bridges and tunnels, illumination, health care, prerequisites for trade and industry, etc., because these are matters of public order and common interest. Likewise, the state organizes a police force and a court system because these are matters of public order and security. I hope you are beginning to understand what public justice involves.

The State and Sexuality

As an example that may further clarify a number of points that I have dealt with so far in this chapter, I choose the domain of sexuality. I said that, because the state only has to maintain public justice, it has nothing to say about what goes on in people's bedrooms. In a state where the authorities are Christians, they personally will be very strongly against all kinds of sexual sins: "Or do you not know that the unrighteous will not inherit the kingdom of God? Do not be deceived: neither the sexually immoral, nor idolaters, nor adulterers, nor men who practice homosexuality, nor thieves, nor the greedy, nor drunkards, nor revilers, nor swindlers will inherit the kingdom of God" (1 Cor. 6:9-10). "For you may be sure of this, that everyone who is sexually immoral or impure, or who is covetous (that is, an idolater), has no inheritance in the kingdom of Christ and God" (Eph. 5:5). Notice the references to the Kingdom of God in these passages!

What the apostle Paul says in these verses is also the personal conviction of authorities who are Christians, or Jews, or Muslims, or other people with high morals. In the community of faith—church, synagogue, mosque—sexual immorality is not to be allowed (cf. 1 Cor. 5). But in the state it is different: not only does the state not have the physical *power* to eliminate all sexual immorality, but it does not have the *authority* to do so either. It is not called upon to permit immorality, in the sense of approving it, but it cannot prohibit it either. If two persons who are not married to each other have sex together *with mutual consent*, the state is not to interfere, even though the authorities, if they have high morals, may *personally* be dead-set against adultery and fornication. It is the primary task of the state to maintain public justice, that is, to protect people against involuntary sex such as rape, sex with minors, trafficking in women selected for involuntary prostitution or pornography.

There may be circumstances in which a state does decide to prohibit prostitution, pornography, and the like. This occurs when the percentage of women working *involuntarily* in the sex industry is estimated to be very high, and when it is hardly possible to distinguish between oppressed and non-oppressed women. In principle, such a prohibition is never for moral reasons as such; the state is not to play the role of moralist. It is not ethically but juridically typified. For the sake of public justice, the state may prohibit prostitution in order to protect women from traffickers, pimps, and pornography producers. Of course, in a civilized country, juridical life unfolds under the guidance of the ethical aspect. But that does not change the fact that laws against prostitution and pornography are basically juridical matters, not ethical matters.

It is not the state that is to morally educate its citizens. Moral education is provided by churches and other faith communities, by humanist associations (if they so wish), in families and in schools with high moral standards (religious or humanist). "My son, . . . [through wisdom] you will be delivered from the forbidden woman, from the adulteress with her smooth words" (Prov. 2:1,16). "Why should you be intoxicated, my son, with a forbidden woman and embrace the bosom of an adulteress?" (Prov. 5:20).

Education and Misunderstandings

Along the same lines of what we just discussed, the state regulates education, not because the state as such loves children so much, but because of the principle of public justice. That is to say, it is righteous to offer to the citizens' children optimal possibilities to acquire knowledge and skills, and to develop their potential. It is a matter of public justice that schools meet certain standards of educational quality, and that inspectors look after this. This is for the benefit not only of the children, but also of the state: the better it educates its young people, the more outstanding will be the citizens it develops.

However, whether this education is best offered to the pupils in a Jewish, a Muslim, a humanist, or a Christian way, is *not* a matter of public justice. This matter is entirely up to the administrators and teachers of the school, and to the parents of the pupils. It is none of the state's business. If politicians argue otherwise, you will find out that this usually occurs because of the following basic misunderstandings. It is worth our while to pay some attention to them:

1. First, there is the mistaken idea that the state's role is *much wider* than that of maintaining public justice. This is what you find in socialism and communism, which assign to the state an all-encompassing function. In its most extreme form, it is the state that determines how parents are to raise their children, how teachers are to educate their pupils, how businessmen have to conduct their business, and even how preachers are to address their congregations.

Please be consistent: if you think the state should not meddle in the internal affairs of families and churches, then the same argument holds for schools. The task of the state does not go any further than that of maintaining public justice: the state must ensure that children are not abused by their parents or teachers, that pupils receive education of good quality, that church congregations do not disturb their neighborhoods, and things like that. *But that's all.* There are no neutral states, just as there are no neutral families, schools, and churches. Christian children are entitled to a *Christian* education at home as well as at school, and to *Christian* preaching in church, and of course the same holds, *mutatis mutandis*, for Jewish, Muslim, Hindu, humanist children, etc.

2. The mistaken idea of a neutral state. Please tell me, where are those neutral authorities? Politicians almost always come from political parties, and these obviously always have a definite ideological color: they may be conservative, or liberal, or socialist, or social-democratic, or Christian-democratic, or communist, or "green," or libertarian, you name it. Within such parties, politicians are recruited for office. These are conservative, or liberal, or socialist, or social-democratic, or Christian-democratic, or communist, or green, or libertarian politicians. Where is the neutrality here?

Now, if there are no neutral states, there definitely are no neutral schools. Teachers, too, are conservative, or liberal, or socialist, or social-democratic, or Christian-democratic, or communist, or green, or libertarian, or humanist, or Jewish, or Muslim, or existentialist, or postmodern, or whatever. Where is the neutrality here?

3. The mistaken idea that the separation between church and state necessarily implies a separation between religion and society. I already underscored that these two separations involve totally different things. I am a great advocate of a strict separation between church and state in the sense of no church denomination dominating the state, and no state dominating any church denomination. At the same time, I claim that the view that religion should have no place in public life is nonsensical. I already gave you my broad circumscription of religion as being any person's ultimate commitment to some Ultimate Ground in which he places his deepest confidence, whatever this Ultimate Ground may be: God, a god, an idol, or an ideology. In this sense, everybody is religious, and the whole state is religious.

You see my point? I do not advocate a greater role for religion in society; rather, I claim that society is religious from top to bottom, from left to right. You see, one can agree with a separation between church and state, and at the same time assert that the whole society is religious, and that therefore the notion of a separation of religion and society is nonsensical. If the state is religious, then of course the school is too. It is my firm opinion that *parents themselves should decide what religion should shape their children's education at school.* Of course, children have to develop an attitude of true tolerance toward other religions and ideologies. But personal religious conviction and religious tolerance go very well together in civilized people.

4. The mistaken idea of the blessings of plurality (called *pluralism* by some). The authorities tell us how beneficial it is for children if, at an early age, they have contact with the plurality of society, that is, with children and teachers of very different traditions and persuasions. My answer to this is, first, let the parents themselves decide whether they think this plurality is beneficial for their children. Why should the authorities be so patronizing

as to tell the parents what is good for their children? Authorities may have an opinion about this, but they cannot and should not impose this opinion on parents. It simply is not their task.

Moreover, secondly, a good school—and inspectors could look after that—does present to its pupils a fair picture of society's plurality. Of course it does. It is the task of a school to prepare its pupils for society. But who could deny to *Christian* (or Jewish, or Muslim, or humanist) parents the right to have their children prepared for a plural society by *Christian* (or Jewish, or Muslim, or humanist, respectively) teachers? Why should Christian parents have to accept that their children must be prepared for society, at the allegedly neutral school, by humanist, communist, atheist, or Muslim teachers? Christians have no problems with humanists, communists, atheists, or Muslims as such, when it comes to human rights and to living peacefully together as human beings. But they do have problems with humanists, communists, atheists, or Muslims, *teaching their young children*. They would rather do that themselves, just like Jewish, Muslim, and humanist parents usually prefer to do that themselves.

The State as a Juridical Institution

We have seen that the state is a juridical institution, whereas marriage, the family, the church, the school, the company, and the association are not. However, I have to repeat that the other societal relationships do all function in the juridical modality (or, do have a juridical aspect). If it were otherwise, the righteousness of God's Kingdom, as far as societal relationships are concerned, could be pursued only in the context of the state. Of course, this is not the case. On the contrary, in actuality the percentage of marriages, families, schools, and companies where the righteousness of God's Kingdom is visibly maintained seems to me to be much greater than the percentage of states where this happens. The state limits itself to maintaining public justice; that is its task. And if it does so explicitly by the light of God's Word, acknowledging God's dominion, then in such a state something of the Kingdom of God becomes manifest, no matter how weakly. But in precisely the same way, the righteousness of God's Kingdom becomes manifest at all places where marriages, families, church denominations or local congregations, schools, companies, associations, parties, etc., function according to the normative standards of God's Kingdom.

However, because only the state is a typically juridical institution, it is the state, and the state alone, that creates the juridical preconditions for the other societal relationships or communities. Note the word *preconditions* here. The state does not meddle in church law (or canon law), that is, the laws that determine internal church life, involving, for instance, matters of church government and church discipline. The state has nothing to say about whether women should be allowed to preach in churches, or whether unrepented sexual offenses are a ground for excommunication. Such matters are entirely decided by the churches themselves. However, as a societal relationship, the church bumps into all kinds of matters of public justice, which do not belong to its own jurisdiction but to that of the state: the permission to buy a certain piece of land to put a church building on it, disruption of church services by outsiders, hindering neighbors through church services (too many cars, too loud music). Also those cases where a church implements mental or physical terror on its (candidate) members, and thus enters the domain of criminal law, are matters that concern all citizens; a matter of public justice and of public order and security.

To repeat: the state maintains the public legal order, in which the rights of other societal relationships are maintained as well. Churches, schools, and companies do not have such a task, only states do. They have the task to keep the many legal interests, both political and non-political, in balance and harmony. Therefore, it is the state, and the state alone, to which the power of the sword has been entrusted (Rom. 13:4, rulers "bear the sword"). Thus, the South African political philosopher, Herman J. Strauss, has defined state authority as a "juridical-integrating dominion authority with a sword monopoly within a limited state territory, in order to serve public justice."

Like all power and authority, this sword monopoly is normative, that is, is determined and constrained by divine norms. Thus, only the state is allowed to enforce its sword power on its citizens by sentencing them to prison—after a fair trial—or even executing them. Church leaders, parents, teachers, employers, administrators, etc., have no sword power over their people. To be sure, parents may punish their children, teachers may punish their pupils, employers may punish their employees (e.g., by not paying bonuses to them), boards may punish the members of their associations (e.g., by excluding them). But they may not imprison such people or execute them; their ways of punishment are restricted by state legislation. Therefore it is the state that interferes when parents punish their children too severely, or when employers fire their employees arbitrarily.

Conversely, the state is not allowed to exceed its authority, for instance, by executing heretics who have been condemned by the church, as happened frequently at the time of the Inquisition (see pp. 6 and 15). Or, if parents are not allowed to punish their children with the sword, the state may not do this for them. Children, pupils, employees, church members, etc., are to be punished *only* by the state if they have violated public criminal law.

Because of this unique position of the state as a juridical relationship, we can have some understanding for the fact that the state so often has been associated in a special way with the Kingdom of God and his righteousness. This is just as misplaced as when people would assign such a role to the church, that is, to a certain church denomination, particularly to the *state church*, as far as such a church still exists in certain countries. The Roman Catholic Church is still the state church in countries like Argentina, Bolivia, Liechtenstein, Monaco, Paraguay, and Peru. The Church of England is the state church in England (but not in the rest of the United Kingdom), the Lutheran Church is still the state church in Denmark and Iceland (not in Sweden and Norway anymore), and the Orthodox Church is the state church in countries like Greece and the Caucasian country of Georgia. It may be understandable if people in such countries would see the Kingdom of God realized in their state, especially in connection with their state church. But this would be erroneous. The Kingdom comes to manifestation—or should come to manifestation—in individual lives as well as in *all* societal relationships; in families, school, companies, etc., just as much as in the state and the church.

People might argue that, of all societal relationships, the church knows best what is God's righteousness and that therefore the church is pre-eminently the place where the Kingdom of God manifests itself. In chapter 6 we will see why this is a big mistake. In no way can God's Kingdom be identified with any societal relationship or community in particular. On the contrary, the Kingdom of God "forcefully advances" in *every* possible societal relationship where righteousness is sought and maintained according to the principles of God's Word and his dominion. We will return to this essential point several times.

Questions for Review

1. Explain and illustrate the notion of sphere sovereignty.

2. Give examples from history of how the state and the church have violated sphere sovereignty.

3. Why is it important not to identify the Kingdom of God with a particular nation state?

4. What is public justice?

5. Explain the juridical aspect of (a) the school or (b) the family. Illustrate ways in which the state maintains public justice toward the societal relationship you choose.

6. Do you believe both of these to be true: (a) that the state may tolerate sexual immorality and (b) government officials may disapprove of sexual immorality? Why (not)?

7. In the Bible, especially the Old Testament, why did God permit things that were wrong?

8. Explain why no school can be religiously neutral.

9. Explain the difference between Christian parochial schools (think of Roman Catholic and many Lutheran schools) and Christian parent-sponsored schools.

10. Why is a "state church" a violation of sphere sovereignty?

CHAPTER THREE

OFFICES AND RESPONSIBILITIES

For every Christian political philosophy, it is of the greatest importance to discern the proper relationship between the various offices and responsibilities, on the one hand, and the Kingdom of God, on the other. I would not know how I could represent this relationship better than with the help of a distinction made by the Dutch Christian philosopher, Dirk H. Th. Vollenhoven (1892-1978). (See my book, *Wisdom For Thinkers*, pp. 75-77.) I refer to the distinction Vollenhoven made between what he called "structure" and "direction."

Structure and Direction

The term *structure* has to do with the creational structures, that is, the structural laws that God has instituted for his numerous creatures, for the societal relationships or communities they form, and for the various cosmic modalities. *Direction* is a dimension that is, so to speak, perpendicular to that of structure; it involves the directedness or orientation of any entity, community, event, or state of affairs. There are many structures, but there are basically only two directions: either the positive orientation toward the Creator and his honor, or the apostate orientation, away from the Creator, to his dishonor. Or, to put it sharply, on the one hand, there is the direction toward the Kingdom of God, on the other hand, the direction to the kingdom of Satan.

   With the help of these two dimensions, structure and direction, we can explain how the fall of Man has changed the *direction* of the human heart. Man's natural, i.e., unredeemed, heart is no longer oriented upon God and his honor, but apostatically (a word related to *apostasy*) directed away from the Creator toward false gods. However, the fall did not change the *structural* dimension of cosmic reality, because that would mean that God's law-order was changed. How could sin change God's own powerful, permanent creational Word, through which he has called the world into existence (the phrase "God said" appears ten times in Gen. 1; Ps. 33:6, 9; Rom. 4:17)? Sin did not alter God's ordinances; what it did alter was the functioning of creatures under these ordinances. If sin had disturbed the law-order as well, this would imply that Man's fall had destroyed the very nature of creation. That would mean that sin and Satan play an autonomous role over against God, a claim that would affect God's very sovereignty. No, God's law-order has not changed—because God has not changed—but Man's functioning under the law has changed for the worse. Structure did not change, but direction did.

Also after the fall, the laws to which reality is subject may still be called "creational ordinances" (a well-known term in Reformed thinking). These ordinances are still the original laws as God instituted them for creation in the beginning. In the manner in which God has maintained the cosmic law-order, also after the fall, his grace and covenantal faithfulness toward fallen humanity come to light. By this faithfulness, he causes the sun to rise on the evil and the good, and sends rain on the righteous and the unrighteous (Matt. 4:45). By this grace, nature and human society after the fall have not been delivered up to the power of evil. As a consequence, they have not fallen apart but remained intact. This grace has been referred to as God's "common grace," to be distinguished from God's "special grace," which comes to light in redemption. There are theological difficulties with this term, but these are beyond the scope of my present study.

Apostasy

In summary, the structures did not change—the direction of the human heart did. The heart has turned away from God and his law. Natural Man may still speak in a linguistically correct way, but his language is basically idolatrous. He still forms proper societal relationships, but their essential religious direction is turned away from God to idols and ideologies. Natural Man still does science, often in a superb way, but his science too is principally directed to false gods. Natural Man and regenerated Man still stand under the same divine law-order, but they live out of different directional heart choices.

In the thinking, speaking, and acting of both groups, the norms and principles of God's law always remain presupposed. But whereas the God-oriented person has chosen obedience to these norms as his life's basis—though in practice he may fail in this—the idol-oriented person lives parasitically off God's law in disobedience. Natural Man is a parasite because, through God's "common grace," God's law sustains his life as well, whereas he attempts to live as if only his own laws hold for him. Sin always presupposes God's law since disobedience to God implicitly refers to divine laws that are not being obeyed. Thus, the harm of, say, lying and stealing, implicitly refers to the norm: "You shall not lie," or "You shall not steal."

The distinction between "structure" and "direction" can help us see how the various offices and responsibilities, on the one hand, and the Kingdom of God, on the other hand, are related to each other. "Structure" refers to the various normative structures that the Creator has laid down in cosmic reality. Just like, for instance, marriage, family, school, and company, the state also has its own structure, pre-given by God, that is, established in God's creational order. Thus, this structure is not autonomously determined by Man, but has a normative character, that is, it stands under God's norms. This pre-given, normative "blueprint" is that which, according to God's ordinances, makes a state to be a state. In other words, a state is a *state* if and only if it answers to the structural law of a state as established in God's creational order.

It will help to understand what I am trying to say if we call these creational structures "horizontal," and call the direction "vertical," because the latter involves the orientation of the societal structures. These structures are either directed towards God as Creator and Lawgiver, to serve and honor him, also within the state, or, as is so often the case after Man's fall, directed away from God, in an apostate direction. In that case, the state is mainly there to serve itself (socialism), or the individual (libertarianism), or "the party" (communism), or "the nation" (*das Volk*; national-socialism), or a certain ideology (all of them).

To a certain extent, we might say that in socialism, the state is deified; in libertarianism, the individual; in communism the party; and in national-socialism, the nation is deified. Only in a truly biblical situation, the state as well as the individual, the party as well as the nation, are directed toward God. We do not serve the state, but the state and we are to serve God. We do not venerate the individual, the party, or the nation; no, both we and the individual, the party, and the nation are to venerate God.

Structure/Direction and the Kingdom

If we correctly grasp "structure" and "direction" as two polarities, as it were, the one perpendicular to the other—that is, not as a dualism!—we will see immediately that the Kingdom of God can never be identified with just one single societal relationship, whichever this may be. In the history of Christian thought, various examples of such false associations can be pointed out. Some people have associated—or even identified—the Kingdom of God especially with the church, others especially with the state, yet others especially with the family.

In this context, I think of the famous Investiture Controversy in medieval Europe (during the eleventh and twelfth centuries, in particular): who was entitled to "invest" (i.e., here, clothe with an official garment) a new bishop: the emperor of the Holy Roman Empire—the highest political figure in Europe—or the pope, the highest spiritual figure in Europe? The emperor said that he had the right to do this because many bishops are "princes" (political chiefs) in their diocese, therefore his vassals. The pope said that he had the right to nominate new bishops because bishops have spiritual offices, and only he could install them in these offices. In other words, this was a battle between the empire and the church. This controversy lasted until the Concordat of Worms (1122) when the matter was solved: the emperor was to install the new bishop as a secular prince in his diocese, and the pope was to install him as a spiritual official in the church.

If you would have asked in those days where the Kingdom of God is most evidently manifest, the adherents of the emperor would have replied, Of course in the *Holy Roman* Empire. The adherents of the pope would have replied, Of course in the *Holy Roman* Catholic Church. In my opinion, they were both wrong, not just in practice, but also in principle. The Kingdom of God has to do with the direction of *each* of the various societal structures *similarly and simultaneously*, not just the state and/or the church. I presume that, during that fight between the emperor and the pope, the Kingdom of God came to far better manifestation in many Christian families, Christian schools, and humble local parishes.

The Lord reigns, not only through the state or the church, but *over* the state and *over* the church, and *over* families, schools, guilds, and today: *over* families, schools, universities, companies, associations, and political parties. It is wrong to suggest that, because the Lord is King, the Kingdom of God is especially associated with the rule of Christian kings, and other Christian government leaders. Too strong a link is then made between the Kingdom of God and the ("Christianized") nation states or empires of this world.

It would be equally wrong, though, to argue that, because we live in an evil world, the Kingdom of God becomes especially manifested in Christian families, which are thought to function as bright spots in a dark world (the third option I mentioned). They do indeed, but genuinely Christian schools where the children attend, the Christian companies where the fathers and/or mothers of such families are employed, and the Christian associations where the fathers and/or mothers are members, are likewise bright spots in a dark world, not to mention faithful local parishes.

"World" and "Society"

The basic error here is the age-old, and almost indelible pietistic mistake of identifying "world" with "society." Avoiding the evil world is then taken to mean, avoiding society. All believers must avoid the world in the vertical sense (direction). This is the world in the meaning it often—not always—has in the Bible: the world of which Satan is the god and the ruler (2 Cor. 4:4; John 12:31; 14:30; 16:11), and where the "cosmic powers over this present darkness" are operating (Eph. 6:12). This is the world that "lies in the power of the evil one" (1 John 5:19; cf. 2:15-17), and to whose "pattern" we should not "conform" (Rom. 12:2).

This is all very important. But often this world is utterly confused with the horizontal dimension: that of the structures. This happens when people tell us that avoiding the world means avoiding certain domains of society, especially politics, universities, trade unions, sport associations, the arts, science, cinemas, theatres, concert halls, and many other forms of social life. I will return to this in chapter 5.

"World" is a vertical concept, which has to do with direction, and not with certain domains of society. "Society" is a horizontal concept, which has to do with structure. It is no use trying to avoid certain societal relationships, because in *every* societal relationship the evil world can manifest itself. This is the same as saying that sin and Satan manifest themselves in it. Do pietists want to avoid the church? I ask this because even in the church the world (that is, "the desires of the flesh and the desires of the eyes and the pride of life," 1 John 2:16) can manifest itself. Do pietists want to avoid the family? Remember, even the family is not safe from the influences of the world. No societal relationship or societal place is *by nature* more worldly than any other: *in itself* the cinema is no more worldly than the church, a sport club no more worldly than the family, a political party no more worldly than a Bible club. In all of these relationships and places, either the kingdom of Satan or the Kingdom of God can manifest itself; there is nothing wrong with them as such—although I have to admit that the Kingdom of God is more likely to be manifested in a Christian family than in any cinema or any nation state.

Decades ago, I myself began being involved in (Christian) politics, and was placed on the list of candidates of a Christian party (either for the national parliament or for the municipal council). To me, it was striking to see how some pietists criticized me for doing that. They blamed me for being involved with the "politics of this world," as some put it. Sometimes these were people who themselves had high positions in society; for instance, they were involved with the "banking of this world," the "companies of this world," the construction of "roads and bridges of this world."

They did not see that the world can manifest itself everywhere, not just in politics, but also in banking—in light of events in recent years we might even say, especially in banking—in business, or whatever activity in society.

Conversely, the Kingdom of God can manifest itself equally in *every* societal relationship or community: in marriages, in families, in churches, in states, in schools, in companies, in associations, in political parties, you name it. None of them is, *by itself*, according to its creational nature, more Kingdom-oriented than the others, *not even the church*. The direction within *each and every* one of these societal relationships manifests itself either in apostasy ("the world"), or in dedication and obedience to God ("the Kingdom of God").

Of course, I do realize that, in practice, we often see a mixture. Sin and Satan can enter Christian families, Christian schools, and Christian congregations through television and the Internet, or even simply through the sinful "flesh" of their members. In every societal relationship, at best only glimpses of the Kingdom of God are manifested. But these glimpses are unspeakably more than nothing, just as even the smallest beam of light means unspeakably more than total darkness.

All Relationships

I repeat: it is of fundamental significance that Jesus Christ rules over all societal relationships. Visibly this is the case in those relationships in which people, through regeneration and the power of the Holy Spirit, acknowledge Christ's authority, and obey his commandments, as is appropriate in the Kingdom of God: we teach to the baptized all the commandments of him who has all authority in heaven and on earth (Matt. 28:18-20). There is such a thing as the "royal law" (James 2:8), that is the law of the Kingdom, the commandments of the King. These are not just the commands that are found explicitly in the New Testament, but they also include, for instance, the creational ordinances that were established in the beginning.

The word "visibly" that I just used does not mean that the King himself becomes visible in the present age. He remains hidden (cf. again Col. 3:3); he is in the "far country" (Luke 19:12). No, "visibly" means that, in such societal relationships, his dominion visibly manifests itself in people who submit to it. Nothing is exempt from his dominion, not even the state. The *whole* world is Christ's Kingdom (cf. Matt. 13:38 with v. 41); angels, authorities, and powers are in submission to him (1 Pet. 3:22). God seated Christ "at his right hand in the heavenly places, far above all rule and authority and power and dominion," already "in this age," and God "put all things under his feet and gave him as head over all things" (Eph. 1:20-22), including the earthly authorities (Rom. 13:1). Therefore, every nation state that, in principle and in practice, functions out of the acknowledgment of Christ's kingship, also within political life, is a manifestation, no matter how weak, of the Kingdom of God.

In the same vein, every family living out of the acknowledgment of Christ's kingship is a manifestation, no matter how weak, of the Kingdom of God. Every marriage in which God's ordinances for marriage are respected is a manifestation of the Kingdom of God; that is, the rule of Christ is recognized in a practical way. Every church denomination and every local church congregation that is ruled by the Word of God, and not by the will of a supposedly autonomous religious Man, is a manifestation of the Kingdom of God. Every Christian school, every Christian company, every Christian association, every Christian political party in which God's Word is acknowledged and Christ's dominion is respected is a manifestation of the Kingdom of God, no matter how weak.

The authority that the Lord has within all societal relationships is delegated to the authorities within each of them. In *marriage*, the husband is the head, to be respected as such by the wife (which will not be difficult for her, if he loves her as Christ loved his church and gave himself for her; Eph. 5:22; Col. 3:18; 1 Pet. 3:1). In the *family*, it is the parents (Eph. 6:1; Col. 3:20). In the *church*, it is the overseers ("bishops") and elders ("presbyters," priests) (1 Tim. 3:1-7; Titus 1:5-9; 1 Thess. 5:12 etc.). In the *state*, it is those who govern (Rom. 13:1-7; Titus 3:1; 1 Pet. 2:13-17).

These are precisely the four institutional relationships that rest upon the divine law-order instituted for the whole of cosmic reality. We have to distinguish them from relationships that have no such direct connection with the divine order, such as the school, the company, the association, and the political party. These are the historical result of a free union of individuals, a union from which one may voluntarily separate. Please note: such voluntary societal relationships do nevertheless have a normative character, that is, they are to be subject to the rules of the Kingdom of God, just like any other societal relationship. I am only saying that we have much more liberty to join them, or to leave them.

Differences

We have distinguished between relationships directly instituted by God: marriage, the family, the Church (with an uppercase C), and the state. Also those that are the outcome of historical developments: church denominations, local congregations, schools, companies, political parties, associations. The differences between these two categories are not to be neglected. They have consequences for the way we respond to authority. Marriage, family, church, and state encompass humans throughout their lives (if we leave out for a moment the divorced, the widowers and widows, the unmarried, the churchless, and the stateless). This means that, within these relationships, we are constantly confronted with authority relationships: between husband and wife, between parent and child, between pastor and church member, between a magistrate and a common citizen.

We can certainly conclude that, apart from everyone's personal obedience to the Master, our obedience within the Kingdom of God is usually manifested primarily in our obedience to the people with authority whom God has placed in marriage, family, church, and state. "For there is no authority except from God, and those that exist have been instituted by God" (Rom. 13:1). Therefore, submitting to the authorities is submitting to God himself. Obedience to God very often simply means nothing but obeying your parents, your elders (pastors, bishop), the state and municipal authorities. Of course, all such authorities can make big mistakes that are unworthy of the Kingdom of God. Only in such cases is there a kind of final escape: we always have to obey God more than humans, whoever they may be (Acts 4:19; 5:29). But this very exceptional case does not change the rule as such; that is, obedience to God involves obedience to the authorities that he has instituted in marriage, family, church, and state.

With societal relationships that are not directly anchored in the divine law-order it is a little different. The institutional relationships encompass my whole life. We cannot step into another marriage just like that (divorce is anti-normative), or into another family, and the switch to another church denomination or to the citizenship of another country is a matter that touches people in their innermost being. Therefore, we are dealing here with a real *bond* of authority, so to speak: I cannot simply replace my spouse, my parents, my elders, or my government by other people. Of course, elders come and go, and governments are regularly replaced by other governments. But that does not change the principle: I am subject to "my elders," or "my government," whoever they may be at a given point in time.

In the non-institutional relationships this is quite different. To be sure, I am obliged to obey on the basis of regulations or contracts: I have committed myself to obedience within the terms of such agreements. But these are *voluntary* agreements: I entered into them of my own free will, and I can leave them of my own free will (at the time and the conditions that the stipulations of this agreement allow me, of course, but I have accepted these conditions beforehand of my own free will). If I am not pleased with my teachers, I can switch to another school. If I am not pleased with my employer, I can look for another job. If the board of my club or political party disappoints me, I might consider cancelling my membership. (Please note again this vital difference: I may not say in a similar way that, if my wife, my children, my church, or my state disappoint me, I am going to look for another wife, other children, another church, or another state.)

Official Authority

Official authority is the authority of "officials," that is, those entrusted with certain "offices." Jesus Christ has official authority in three respects because of his threefold office as Mediator: as

King, Priest, and Prophet. Authority is always linked with, and restricted to, a certain office. In a family, the father is not to play the elder, even if he is an elder in church, or to play the statesman in his home, even if he is a statesman in the government, but to be the *father*. He has to exercise his authority in accordance with the nature of his fatherly office. If he is a policeman, he exercises that office out on the street, not at home. Official authority is normative: the person who trespasses the limits of his office acts in an anti-normative way.

At the same time, it is true that those who neglect their office also act in an anti-normative way. Every office implies a divine calling, which has to be carried out. An office is not just an honorary title, but involves *work* to be done. If you are a parent, a spouse, an elder, a state official, *do* something about it! A husband only "earns" the respect of his wife by the most loving dedication (Eph. 5:22-29; Col. 3:19; 1 Pet. 3:7). A parent should not embitter his/her children, but raise them for the Lord, and for the benefit of the children, not for the parent's own interests (Eph. 6:4; Col. 3:21). Elders and pastors must protect and feed the flock of which the *Holy Spirit* has made them overseers (Acts 20:28); they are not to exploit or tyrannize the flock (1 Pet. 5:2-3). State and municipal authorities must rule for the benefit of the citizens (Rom. 13:4). The best kings are those who love and serve the King, and who view their service toward others in this light.

Thus, fulfilling an office never primarily serves one's own interests but those of others. Jesus Christ is our great example: he who "confers" a Kingdom to us (as he puts it) said, "The kings of the Gentiles exercise lordship over them, and those in authority over them are called benefactors. But not so with you. Rather, let the greatest among you become as the youngest, and the leader as one who serves. For who is the greater, one who reclines at table or one who serves? Is it not the one who reclines at table? But *I am among you as the one who serves*" (Luke 22:25-30, italics added; cf. Eph. 5:22-23). "The Son of Man came not to be served, but to serve" (Matt. 20:28). This is what official authority entails according to God's principles: it is dominion, but always serving dominion. It is not serving one's own interests, or those of one's friends (nepotism), but the interests of the people entrusted to the "official," to the honor of God. In all authority exercised in this biblical way *something of the Kingdom of God is manifested.*

Let me come back here to the exception mentioned in Acts 4:19 ("Which is right in God's eyes: to listen to you [authorities], or to him?") and 5:29 ("We must obey God rather than human beings"). This is a biblical principle, and therefore perfectly true— but it is a principle that can very easily be abused. Wives must respect their husbands, even if they are disobedient husbands (1 Pet. 3:1). Children, pupils, and church members must obey their parents, their teachers, and their elders and pastors, respectively, even if these "officials" sometimes badly misbehave. Even a wicked state official like the emperor Nero had to be obeyed (Rom. 13:1-7). Slaves and servants must obey their masters, even if the latter are harsh (1 Pet. 2:18). Therefore, Christians have to be very careful when they appeal to the principle that "God has to be obeyed more than human beings."

Between a Rock and a Hard Place

The exception of Acts 4:19 and 5:29 is only a *last resort,* applicable only if obedience to authorities would entail outright disobedience to God. A simple example may suffice. If I had to send my children to a state school where they would be exposed to all kinds of apostate thinking—perhaps under the cover of allegedly neutral teaching—a situation might come up in which I would have to say: That's the limit. I would need legal advice as to what I could possibly do in such a situation. Home schooling might be a possibility. But the social environment of a school is usually to be preferred to the private atmosphere of home schooling.

So what are the options? They may differ from country to country, from situation to situation, from parent to parent, and from child to child. But parents may sense that they are between a rock and a hard place as they observe with great sorrow what kinds of sinful thinking their children are exposed to at the state school.

I repeat here what I said before: no state authorities, no journalists, no philosophers, not even theologians and church officials, are to tell the parents what constitutes "sinful thinking," and what level of "sinful thinking"—sometimes covered up as allegedly neutral thinking—parents still ought to consider to be acceptable for their children. *It is up to the parents, and to no one else*, to decide that for their children. These are *their* children, not the state's, or the church's. Of course, other people might help to inform the parents in this respect, help them to develop their own thinking, advise them, encourage them to develop more tolerance, or on the contrary, to find the courage to protest. But in the end, it is the parents who decide.

It is the wish—or even a fundamental principle—of many Christian (and Jewish, and Muslim, etc.) parents that the school be an extension of the Christian (or Jewish, or Muslim, etc.) home. The younger the children are, the more sensitive and receptive they are, and the more the parents will demand that the Christian (or Jewish, or Muslim, etc.) atmosphere of the home is extended to the school. What they teach their children at home they do not want to see being demolished at school. When the children are grown up, they can and will decide for themselves. But as long as they are immature, it is the *responsibility* of all parents—Christians and non-Christians—to see to it that their children are educated at school in a way similar to that at home.

Parents may be wrong—Christians have other ideas about education than Jews, Muslims, and humanists—*but no one can decide that for them* in a patronizing way. If parents are wrong, they will have to find that out themselves, or their children will, in due time, find that out for themselves. No outside authority has any right to interfere in this process. The only exception is parents who tyrannize their children, abuse them, physically or mentally. Then it is a matter of *protecting* the children against the parents, both physically and mentally. But authorities must be extremely reluctant to judge a family situation to be such an exceptional case. Unfortunately, today it is happening more and more in North America that parents who wish to decide about their children's education according to their Christian worldview are "diagnosed" as mentally abusing their children! This is putting the world upside down. It reminds us of Roman Catholic France, which after 1685 took the children away from Protestant parents, or of the communist countries in Eastern Europe, where children

43

of Christian parents were taken away, in both cases to educate them according to the ruling religion or ideology. It is an early indication of the inclination to totalitarianism.

Questions for Review

1. Explain the meaning of the terms *structure* and *direction*.

2. Illustrate the impact of humanity's fall into sin upon both *structure* and *direction*.

3. "The Kingdom of God is identical to the Church." True or false? Why?

4. Explain, with reference to the Bible, the differences between the "world" and "society."

5. Put in your own words what it means that the Kingdom of God can be manifested in Christian marriage.

6. Explain the distinction between societal relationships that rest on the law-order instituted for all of creation, and societal relationships that arose in history.

7. Explain why the distinction you explained for Question 6 is important for Christian living in the world.

8. Think about all the many relationships that you have. Illustrate several "offices" that you hold, and mention some ways in which you exercise those offices.

9. From what you've learned in this chapter, evaluate this claim: "The education of a child is a responsibility that belongs primarily, though not exclusively, to the child's parents."

Chapter Four

THEOCRACY

The issue of *theocracy* has always been a knotty problem in any discussion about Christian politics, and the confusion it creates has often been tremendous. Some Christians reject the notion of theocracy out of hand because of the very negative connotations it has. They are reminded of Christian theologians or philosophers who, according to them, handled the notion of theocracy in a very wrong way. Let me give just one example of one of the common misunderstandings in relation to theocracy. People argue, "Theocracy literally means 'divine power,' and democracy means 'the people's power.' The two are radically opposed: it is either God who reigns, or it is the people who reign. You cannot have both. Theocracy is God's ideal, and therefore also the Christian's ideal. Therefore, Christians should be opposed to democracy."

Nothing could be further from the truth than this kind of reasoning. I firmly believe in theocracy, and I firmly believe in democracy. To me, the two are not at all contradictory, or mutually exclusive. I think it is one of the challenges, as well as one of the benefits, of a Christian politicology (the study of political systems) to sort out misunderstandings like this one.

By the way, today there hardly seems to be a problem anymore. Even the strictest Christians nowadays accept the democratic system, just like many very strict Jews in Israel accept it. This acceptance comes to light in strict Christians as well as Jews joining existing political parties, or forming their own parties, with which they take part in the democratic system of their respective countries. However, this does not mean that all orthodox Christians or Jews could *explain* why they, as advocates of theocracy, have no difficulty with the democratic system. They cannot *account* for this seeming discrepancy. This is where a biblical politicology (political science) comes in.

Misunderstanding

Of course, the confusion between theocracy and democracy is created by the fact that the two terms both end with the suffix -*cracy*. Therefore, they seem to belong to the same category, which is not the case at all. Democracy is a form of state government, just like aristocracy (Plato's ideal) and nomocracy (the medieval church state). Theocracy, however, just like technocracy, bureaucracy, ochlocracy (supremacy of the crowd, "mob rule"), dominocracy (supremacy of church pastors), ergatocracy (supremacy of the workers), and gynecocracy (supremacy of women), are not serious political forms of government. They are disparate because they belong to incomparable categories.

To be more precise: theocracy and democracy relate to one another as *direction* relates to *structure* (you will remember everything I said about this distinction before). Within the normative ground-structure that, according to God's creational ordinances, makes a state to be a state, several different state *forms* are possible, of which democracy is only one. The great Dutch historian and politician, Guillaume Groen van Prinsterer (1801-1876), was for many years a member of the Dutch parliament. In his famous work, *Unbelief and Revolution*, he argued that, for a Christian politicology, what is decisive is not the state *form* as such—although some forms are definitely better than others—but the extent to which, within a given state form, God's commandments are observed. In our terms, what is decisive for a Christian political science is not primarily the *structure* of the state, but its *direction*, its spiritual orientation, toward God, or toward sin and Satan; that is, the extent to which the Kingdom of God comes to manifestation in the state.

As I said, on the one hand, every state has a ground-*structure* that makes a state to be a state. Within the boundaries of that ground-structure, there are many forms that Man, in his responsibility to God, can give to the state. Democracy is one of these forms. On the other hand, theocracy has to do with the *direction* of the state, not with its form. Whether we have to do with an absolute monarchy, or an aristocracy, or a democracy, in all these cases the state is either *theocratically* oriented (*theos* = God), that is, acknowledging God's authority, formally and practically, or it is *anthropocratically* oriented (*anthropos* = Man), that is, allegedly autonomous Man is ruling himself, to his own honor. Thus, theocracy and democracy are not opposites. On the contrary, a theocratic, that is theocratically oriented, democracy is quite conceivable, and in the present age, to many Christians it is even desirable. This is a democracy that is governed by a theocratic attitude, i.e., by the recognition that God is in charge, and by submission to his Word.

In the sense in which I have circumscribed it here, the terms "theocracy" and "Kingdom of God" are almost interchangeable. The only difference is that theocracy is a very general reference to God's universal government, in which the historical-eschatological dimension is lacking that is so characteristic of the term "Kingdom of God." The latter does not refer only to the general dominion of God, but also to the way God is moving forward toward the "end of the age," the time when all enemies will be made a footstool for the feet of Christ (Heb. 1:13), the "world to come," which will be laid under the feet of the Son of Man (Heb. 2:5-8), the progress of Christ's dominion until God will be "all in all" (1 Cor. 15:24-28). Bible-believing Christians have many different views on eschatology; these differences are of no concern to us now. The only point that matters right now is that they all agree on this eschatological character of the Kingdom of God.

Of course, we do not want to speak naïvely of a "theocratic democracy," that is, a democracy with a theocratic attitude, or directed by theocratic norms. We do realize that present-day democracy is by and large a product of Enlightenment humanism. Therefore, the question might arise as to whether a typically humanistic state structure *a priori* harbors the possibility of ever assuming a theocratic orientation. The answer is that only in the nineteenth century, modern Western democracy acquired its typically humanistic form. Before that time, Christian thinking put a mark on the development of democracy that was at least as great as that of humanism.

Besides, the earliest roots of democracy were already found in the societal structure of the ancient Germanic nations, with their ideas of personal freedom and personal rights. They had their local, representative public meetings of free men, which already before the Renaissance brought forth the English parliament. They also elected their own kings, a custom that for centuries lived on in the election of the German emperor, although they also knew of hereditary kings.

Popular Sovereignty

The most humanistic element in modern democratic thinking is the notion of "popular sovereignty," or "people's sovereignty." That is, the highest authority in society is "we the people." It is no wonder that many believe in a contrast between theocracy and democracy because of the misleading meaning of democracy itself. If theocracy means that God (*theos*) is in charge, then democracy means the people (*demos*) are in charge. Historically speaking, the term *democracy* certainly has this background. However, that does not mean that the Christian who is a supporter of democracy necessarily is an adherent of the notion of popular sovereignty. On the contrary, we can definitely give a Christian content to the term *democracy*, at the same time firmly rejecting the notion of people's sovereignty. The people are not sovereign, nor is any council of ministers.

Even the sovereignty of a "sovereign" is only derived sovereignty. The fact that the parliament is chosen by the people does not turn voters into rulers or authorities; on the contrary, voters always remain *under* authority. The authority of the government and the right to vote are not at all the same. The right to vote is only the right to place certain persons in a position of authority, and afterward to evaluate how the latter have accomplished their job. The right to vote is not the right to exercise authority, the right to rule.

Moreover, as I said, even the highest authority of those in authority is at best derived authority. The Lord God is the only absolute Sovereign recognized by the Christian. He rules over our personal lives, as well as over the societal relationships in which we share. He rules through the authorities that belong to every societal relationship: through state and city authorities, through elders and bishops, through parents and principals, etc. These authorities are never sovereign themselves because they have only derived authority. The Lord alone is sovereign.

The God who appoints authorities does so through the historical relationships in which people live. In other words, he does it *providentially*. Divine appointment is transcendent, but it is realized in an immanent way: authorities arise out of historical circumstances. They come forth from tribal wars, from revolutions, from internal power struggles, from conquests, from political marriages, from aristocratic or democratic elections. But in whatever way they may have come to power, as a matter of principle these authorities must be accepted as appointed by God, as servants of God (Rom. 13:1, 4). This is so even if tribal wars, revolutions, and the like as such presuppose the wickedness of natural Man. By the way, this wickedness is the very reason why democracy is the "least bad" of all political forms: it is the political system that offers the best guarantee that no single group will get all the power in its hands but that all will listen to one another, all are obliged to work together, and all interest groups keep each other in balance.

Aristocracy

If I call democracy the "least bad' political form, this has to be understood in a correct way. Just like the term "the best" does not necessarily imply "good"—the best of a few bad things is still bad—the term "the least bad" does not necessarily imply "bad." Therefore, I could just as well have said democracy is "the best political form"; at least, that is the kind of democracy found in countries with a certain level of civilization, sufficient social differentiation, individual maturity, sufficient responsibility for people's own cultural inheritance, etc.

So why do I prefer the term "least bad"? In this expression, the dream continues to resonate that, at first sight, an aristocracy is always more attractive. That is, a government of magistrates who did not rise to power through their personal ambition or their popularity, or through the political self-interest of a certain majority of the people, but purely because they are the best, the wisest, the most intelligent, the most expert, and especially the most unselfish.

How wonderful would that be! This would be a government

that does not rule by the grace of its constituency, whose leaders do not always have the next election on their minds. On the contrary, it is a government that can do the best for its people, not just that for which there is sufficient political support, that which is politically achievable. This ideal government does not live out of ideologies, and does not flounder in confusion when ideologies are everywhere discredited, but is elevated above the whims of all ideologies.

Alas, such an aristocracy does not exist. In the end, every so-called aristocracy leads to tyranny and terror. All Napoleons and Hitlers, who, as people say, "did so much good for their own people," ended as foreshadowings of the Antichrist. True aristocracy lies in the vertical dimension of the Kingdom of God; that is, in the dominion of the *aristos*, the Very Best. As long as the Messiah has not returned, democracy is always the horizontal political form that is far to be preferred to any appearance of aristocracy. Or, to put it a little differently, under the present circumstances, theocratically oriented democracy *is* a form of aristocracy: a government by the Very Best, albeit by means of defective human instruments.

Even a "government of national unity," which we sometimes encounter in countries with many different political parties, must be reserved for emergency situations, because it operates without the healthy counter-balance of an "opposition." Such a balance of forces belongs to the very essence of a democracy; it is the best guarantee for harmony and stability. Throughout the ages, Christians have never enjoyed a more "peaceful and quiet life" (1 Tim. 2:2) than in truly democratically ruled countries. But I repeat: from a Christian point of view, democracy never involves popular sovereignty. The latter notion implies that the authorities are a kind of "employees" of the people (the "employer"), somewhat like king Saul, who said, "I feared the people and obeyed their voice" (1 Sam. 15:24). Ideally speaking, the authorities are not employed by the people, but by God. Before anything else, they are bound to the commandments of the Kingdom of God.

In this sense, *every* democracy is necessarily a theocratic democracy because in every state, whatever its political form may be (its *structure*), the Lord reigns, whether the majority of the citizens acknowledge this or not (its *direction*). Theocracy is not a kind of ideal of God that should be realized by his believing children, just as the Kingdom of God is not a kind of ideal that will be realized only at the second coming of Christ. Already now, the Kingdom of God is "forcefully advancing," namely, in all places where people and societal relationships explicitly put themselves under the dominion of Christ and his Word. To be sure, today sin is still reigning on this earth (Rom. 6:12), and Satan is still the god of this world (2 Cor. 4:4). But that does not alter the fact that the Kingdom of God is "forcefully advancing." Behind the scenes, it is God who is reigning. Even sin and Satan's work can take place only under God's permission; willy-nilly they are instruments in his hand.

Ancient Israel

It would not be correct, I think, to say that theocracy is an ideal that was better realized in Old Testament Israel than in our present-day democracies. I make this claim because the Lord can reign just as well though a weak, sinful, absolute monarch (David, Solomon, etc.) as through a weak, sinful government in a present-day democracy. The most important differences with ancient Israel are not to be found in the political form as such—absolute monarchy versus a parliamentary democracy (such as in the United Kingdom and Canada) or a presidential democracy (such as in France and the United States)—but in several other points.

(1) The monarchs in ancient Israel, at least those from the house of David, were appointed directly by God, through prophets who received and declared his will. Think of the prophet Samuel, who anointed Saul (1 Sam. 10:1), and later David (16:13). All the next kings of Judah came forth from the house of David as a hereditary "automatism," but even then, spiritual leaders sometimes directly voiced the will of God with respect to the choice of the king (e.g., 2 Kings 11).

(2) A practical difference is to be found, not in structure, but in direction: out of the house of Judah came a number of kings who "did what was right in the eyes of the LORD" (1 Kings 15:5, 11; 22:43; 2 Kings 12:2; 14:3; 15:3, 34; 18:3; 22:2), even though in the end they all failed badly. In our modern democracies, however, there have been only a few governments that publicly and earnestly

sought the will of the Lord, and thereby embodied the notion of a theocratically oriented democracy.

(3) Israel had a very special position as a people standing in a covenantal relationship with God. Therefore, as a nation it was called to keep all idolatry and false religion outside its national borders. At *that* time, that was a task of the state because a national interest was involved; in other words, it was a matter of public justice. Today, however, no nation *as a nation* stands in a covenantal relationship with God (I leave present-day ethnic Israel or the modern state of Israel out of consideration; that is a nut for the theologians to crack). On the contrary, God is gathering a people for himself *out of all the nations* (Acts 15:14; cf. Rom. 9:24-25; Titus 2:14; 1 Pet. 2:9). (I say this in spite of the famous Reformed slogan, "God, Netherlands and Orange," which was the name of electoral clubs led by Groen van Prinsterer in the nineteenth century.) Therefore, expelling false religion and idolatry is no longer a matter of public justice, and thus not the task of the state (see below).

It is a task of the church, though, to do this. However, it has only one weapon at its disposal: not the literal sword, but the sword of the Spirit, that is, the Word of God (Eph. 6:17). Where a close link between the Christian church and the allegedly Christian state is assumed, notions such as a "national church" (German *Volkskirche*; Dutch: *volkskerk*) or a "baptized nation" (Philippus J. Hoedemaker: *gedoopte natie*) have originated, notions with which I have great difficulty, both theologically and politicologically.

The comparison with the God-given monarchy in ancient Israel does not imply a condemnation of democracy as a political form, as not being God-given. It is not *structure* that is to be condemned but the *direction* of the human heart, which should shape democracy in a theocratic way. What answers more to God's ideal: the absolute-monarchic Judah under, for instance, wicked king Ahaz, formally appointed by God (2 Kings 16; 2 Chron. 28), or a democracy led by a Bible-believing government? In which of the two does the Kingdom of God come to manifestation more clearly? The opposite is true, too: a state is not good because it is democratic, but because it accomplishes its God-given task well, that is, the task of maintaining public justice the way God intended it to be (even if the government of that state does not formally or publicly acknowledge God).

From the viewpoint of *structure*, a democracy is better than any other political form. From the viewpoint of *direction*, the best state is the one honoring God, whatever its political form may be. But, I repeat, objectively speaking, even a state, no matter its political form, which explicitly dishonors God is fundamentally theocratic because even in such a state, God is and remains the sovereign ruler behind the scenes. Theocracy is both: it is a principal (objective) matter: the Lord reigns, whatever the attitude of a government may be. It is also an ideal (subjective) matter: the theocratic ideal comes to manifestation in a state, whatever its political form may be, that honors God and keeps his commandments. In such a state we see glimpses of the Kingdom of God.

Ecclesiocracy?

Some people have suggested that a so-called theocratic political form involves the church having supremacy over the state. This again is a confusion of structure and direction. The underlying error usually is that, in some way or another, the church is considered to be nearer to the Kingdom of God than any of the other societal relationships. The basic mistake here is the confusion between the Church as the eternal-transcendent Body of Christ (e.g., Eph. 1-3) and the church in its historical-immanent form as a "denomination," or a set of "denominations," on earth. In this historical-immanent form, "the" church—more correctly, a certain church denomination, or a local church congregation—is one societal relationship among many others.

The practical significance of this distinction between the church and the Kingdom of God can be easily explained. Just ask yourself the question: Does the Kingdom of God manifest itself in a certain church denomination, or in a local church congregation, in a better, higher, clearer way than in any other societal relationship? Does not the Kingdom of God manifest itself more gloriously in many Christian marriages, families, schools, companies, associations, and political parties, than in certain (back-sliding) church denominations? Sometimes, churches harbor evils that in other societal relationships would not even be tolerated (cf. 1 Cor. 5:1)! Of course, to me, a local church congregation, because of its structural nature, has more spiritual substance than, for instance, a local sports club or a trade union. But I also know that some of these latter associations look after their own people better than certain church congregations do. In no way are we ever allowed to place "the church"—that is, a certain church denomination, or a local church congregation—above any of the other societal relationships or communities.

Where "the church"—or a body of Muslim spiritual leaders, for that matter, as in Iran—has the supremacy over the state, democracy is replaced by what we could call an "ecclesiocracy." This is a state that is ruled by a certain church denomination (usually a "state church," or a "national church"), or ruled by whatever other religious body, like a group of *ayatollahs*. Please note, however, that both democracy and ecclesiocracy have to do with structure, not with direction. That is to say, in a state dominated by some church denomination (as with a "state church"), the Kingdom of God does not automatically come to manifestation more clearly than, for instance, in a democracy. The reason is that the manifestation of the Kingdom of God is a matter of direction, not structure.

It is not difficult to grasp this: in principle, a democracy can very well be theocratically oriented—in the way I have described—whereas an ecclesiocracy can very well be anthropocratically oriented by church (or other religious) leaders governing the state in their own arbitrary way, for their own honor, without factually respecting God's Word and the dominion of Christ.

Therefore, an ecclesiocracy as such does not necessarily make the state more theocratic than, for instance, a democracy. The reason is that the whole matter of theocracy has nothing to do with the state's political form as such. Theocracy has to do with the attitude of human hearts. In other words, the question whether, for instance, a democracy is more desirable than an ecclesiocracy has nothing to do with theocracy but with understanding God's ordinances for society.

In a certain sense, an ecclesiocracy would, by definition, not be very theocratic because it would be a denial of the very ordinances of God for society, namely, those implying distinct offices and responsibilities. I mean, the church does preach justification by faith but is not responsible for maintaining public justice. The former is part of the church's task, the latter is not. Maintaining public justice is the responsibility of the state. Church leaders are not to be confused with state leaders.

Belgic Confession, Article 36

Our considerations to this point have interesting implications with respect to Article 36 of the Belgic Confession (1561), written by the Walloon theologian, Guido de Brès, who died as a martyr in 1567. This Confession has been formally accepted by Reformed churches worldwide. In the original version of Article 36, we read that the office of the magistracy is, among other things, to "remove and prevent all idolatry and false worship." Some people have felt that to retain these words would reflect a more theocratic view of the state than to omit these words. In my opinion, this is a mistake. It would *not* be theocratic at all if the state would (ab)use its power of the sword to "remove and prevent all idolatry and false worship." This would be wrong in principle and in practice.

It is wrong in principle, because the state would go beyond its authority if it went beyond the strict domain of public justice and entered into the arena of the individuals' personal beliefs and the internal domain of religious communities. Such a state would be disobedient to divine ordinances, and thus in fact would not display a theocratic attitude at all. It is *not* the duty or authority of the state to Christianize the whole of society—even if it were at all able to do so.

Also in practice the original wording of Article 36 is to be rejected. This is because, if these words were retained, any Christian subcommunity of believers would have to fear that, one day, a certain government, likely led by some "state church" or guided by some "state religion," would judge that *their* views represent "idolatry and false worship," and that, therefore, *they* should be expelled. No religious group would be safe anymore!

This is why the Protestant Reformed Churches in America have added the following note to the quoted words from Article 36: "This phrase, touching the office of the magistracy in its relation to the Church, proceeds on the principle of the Established Church, which was first applied by Constantine and afterwards also in many Protestant countries. History, however, does not support the principle of State domination over the Church, but rather the separation of Church and State. Moreover, it is contrary to the New Dispensation that authority be vested in the State to arbitrarily reform the Church, and to deny the Church the right of independently conducting its own affairs as a distinct territory alongside the State. The New Testament does not subject the Christian Church to the authority of the State that it should be governed and extended by political measures, but to our Lord and King only as an independent territory alongside and altogether independent of the State, that it may be governed and edified by its office-bearers and with spiritual weapons only. Practically all Reformed churches have repudiated the idea of the Established Church, and are advocating the autonomy of the churches and personal liberty of conscience in matters pertaining to the service of God."

This is also why Belgic Confession, Article 36 was debated several times in the history of the Christian Reformed Church in North America (in 1910, 1938, and 1958). In 1958, the following note was added: "In the original text this sentence read as follows: 'Their office is not only to have regard unto and watch for the welfare of the civil state, but also that they protect the sacred ministry, and thus may remove and prevent all idolatry and false worship, that the kingdom of antichrist may be thus destroyed and the kingdom of Christ promoted.' The Christian Reformed Church Synod of 1910, recognizing the unbiblical teaching, contained in this sentence, concerning the freedom of religion and concerning the duty of the state to suppress false religion, saw fit to add an explanatory footnote. The Christian Reformed Church Synod of 1938, agreeing with the Christian Reformed Church Synod of 1910 as to the unbiblical character of the teaching referred to, but recognizing a conflict between the objectionable clauses in the Article and its footnote, decided to eliminate the footnote and to make the change in the text of the Article which appears above, corresponding to the change adopted in 1905 by the General Synod of the 'Gereformeerde Kerken in Nederland.' The Christian Reformed Church Synod of 1958 approved the following substitute statement which has been referred to other Reformed Churches accepting the Belgic Confession as their creed for evaluation and reaction: 'And being called in this manner to contribute to the advancement of a society that is pleasing to God, the civil rulers have the task, in subjection to the law of God, while completely refraining from every tendency toward exercising absolute authority, and while functioning in the sphere entrusted to them and with the means belonging to them, to remove every obstacle to the preaching of the gospel and to every aspect of divine worship, in order that the Word of God may have free course, the kingdom of Jesus Christ may make progress, and every anti-Christian power may be resisted.'"

Interestingly, both of these supplementary notes refer almost explicitly to the notion of sphere sovereignty as originally formulated by Abraham Kuyper, and rightly so.

Questions for Review

1. In light of this chapter, how would you define *theocracy*?

2. Can you explain how it is possible to defend both theocracy and democracy.

3. Define "popular sovereignty," and explain how a Christian can both defend democracy and reject popular sovereignty.

4. Explain why Christians should defend *theocracy* in terms of *direction* but not in terms of *structure*.

5. In what sense is an "aristocracy" desirable, and in what sense is it not?

6. What differences do you see between the political form of ancient Israel and present-day political forms?

7. Why is a democracy with a theocratic orientation preferable to an ecclesiocracy?

8. Explain why the revision of Belgic Confession, Article 36, was necessary.

Chapter Five

Strangers and Pilgrims

In the Old Testament God told the people of Israel, "The land is mine. For you are strangers and sojourners with me" (Lev. 25:23; cf. 1 Chron. 29:15; Ps. 39:13). The apostle Paul tells the Gentile Christians, "You are no longer strangers and sojourners" (Eph. 2:19, ESV note), but this was what they were in relation to the believers from Israel. At the same time it was right what Peter says, "Beloved, I urge you as sojourners and exiles to abstain from the passions of the flesh, which wage war against your soul" (1 Pet. 2:11; cf. 1:1, "To those who are elect exiles of the Dispersion. . ."). And the epistle to the Hebrews presents to the believers the example of the patriarchs, who recognized "that they were strangers and exiles on the earth. . . . For people who speak thus make it clear that they are seeking a homeland. . . they desire a better country, that is, a heavenly one" (Heb. 11:13-16).

The "World"

The believer is a "foreigner," an "exile," a "stranger" on earth, or, as some would say, a "pilgrim," that is, someone traveling through a strange country to some holy place. This means that the regenerated, believing person realizes that he finds himself in the midst of, and over against, a world that is strongly dominated by sin, Satan, and death. By nature, the believer is "foreign" to this evil world, whereas at the same time he stands right in the middle of this world. He stands there with a calling he has to fulfill in this very world. As a "pilgrim," he is on his way, traveling through the present world, to another, better world, the holy world of God and his Christ.

It may seem strange to deal with this Christian notion of *pilgrimage* in a treatise on Christian politicology. Some pietistic

Christians have used this very notion of pilgrimage to reject the whole idea of Christian politics—"we have nothing to seek in this world"—or to reject any Christian participation in politics. "Foreigners don't vote in the country where they sojourn." It is my opinion that the very opposite is true: the Christian notion of being foreigners may help us to get a clearer idea of the position of Christians in society, and of their proper attitude towards politics.

First, we must get a clear picture of the meanings of the word *world*. Sometimes, this word has quite a neutral meaning in the Bible. In these cases, it means the whole of creation (e.g., Matt. 4:8; Rom. 1:20), or of humanity (e.g., John 3:16; Mark 14:9). But in many cases, the word *world* has a negative meaning: it is the system of sin and Satan (besides the verses quoted earlier in chapter 3, see Rom. 3:19; 1 Cor. 3:19; Gal. 1:4; 6:14; 2 Tim. 4:10). When Jesus says that his followers are still "in the world" (John 17:11), the word may still have more or less a neutral meaning. But when he adds that they are not "of the world" (vv. 14-16), then *world* is this negative realm of sin and Satan to which believers do not belong.

It is very important to distinguish between the two meanings. Christians are "in the world," that is, they not only live on the same planet as the wicked, but they are part of the same society. They take part in it as employers and employees, as buyers and sellers, as citizens and taxpayers, they take part in street traffic, in business life, in the world of science, in cultural life, etc. All of this has to do with the structure of this world. But *world* in the other, negative meaning has to do with direction. In the former, horizontal sense, we are definitely *not* foreigners and exiles: we may be proud of our earthly country, we may be happy with the place we occupy in society. We may take part in it to the full, and find a lot of satisfaction in it, for which we are thankful to the Lord. In the latter, vertical sense, however, we realize that we *are* foreigners and exiles: we do not want to have anything to do with the world as the domain of sin and Satan (although, unfortunately, we cannot always avoid them). Taking the two dimensions together, we might say, "There is nothing we have to fear in society except sin and Satan" (Herman Dooyeweerd).

Separatism

It is quite understandable that, in church history, the notion of Christians being foreigners has often led to what the Dutch call *wereldmijding*, that is, "avoiding the world" through world flight, separatism, and quietism. In this way, the two meanings of *world* were totally confused, that is, structure and direction were mixed up. There is no single domain in this world that as such is false, as long as its direction is upward.

Those who misunderstood this began to avoid certain *domains* in society, as if these domains in themselves were false: politics, universities, sport clubs, trade unions, the arts, music, science, etc. They did not see that any of these domains—without exception— could either be consecrated to God, or become subservient to sin and Satan. None of these domains are wrong in themselves—it is only their direction that may be very false. The latter holds for *all* societal domains, including marriage, the family, and even the church—they all might become apostate! The power of sin and Satan is not by definition stronger in one societal relationship than in any other. If people want to "avoid the world" in the sense I have just described, they would be consistent only if they would withdraw from *all* societal relationships and communities (cf. 1 Cor. 5:10).

However, even withdrawing into a convent (monastery, nunnery) would not help, because the convent, too, is a societal community in which sin and Satan can manifest themselves. Even any church denomination, or any local church congregation, would not be safe because sin and Satan may manifest themselves there no less than in any other societal relationship (cf. Christ's complaints against five of the seven churches in Rev. 2 and 3). This is because in every social structure there are people who live in terms of the "flesh" (their sinful nature). Anyone wanting to withdraw from the world would, as it were, have to withdraw from himself, for the world manifests itself in our own hearts. It is not just an enemy out there, it is an enemy that finds an ally, a "fifth column," within ourselves.

The very same holds for the opposite: the Holy Spirit manifests himself primarily in the hearts and lives of individual believers, and subsequently in the societal relationships and communities to which these believers belong. No societal relationships are by themselves evil or worldly, because each of them is rooted in God's creational ordinances. Therefore, if some societal relationships would be evil in themselves, we would have to blame God's creational law for these relationships! No, it is not the God-given structures that are bad, it is only their direction that can be bad because of sinful people functioning in them. To these structures belong faithful, dedicated churches, as well as apostate cultural and scientific associations—to state the matter in black-and-white—just as there are also corrupt, apostate churches as well as cultural and scientific associations dedicated to God. The structures as such are never bad—it is their direction that can be very bad.

"Sacred" and "Profane"

The whole coupling of our pilgrimage to some form of "avoiding the world," in the sense of avoiding (parts of) society or avoiding (parts of) culture, is *a priori* mistaken. The basic error is linking that which is sinful, evil, and unholy with certain areas in life and in society that are to be avoided. This is a relic of medieval scholastic thinking, in which nature—the allegedly profane domain—is separated from grace, the sacred domain. This error occurred in strict Roman Catholic circles with their various forms of asceticism, especially in convents. It occurred in very conservative (paleo-) Reformed circles where almost the whole of society seemed taboo and was left to the enemy. It occurred in Anabaptist circles where, in its most extreme form, the German city of Münster at a certain moment was the safe haven for God's people (1535). It occurred in neo-Calvinist circles with their strong emphasis on their own entirely independent Christian organizations in every domain of life. These are very different religious denominations, but with one common error: the idea that there are sacred domains and there are profane domains. To such Christians, "Do not be conformed to this world" (Rom. 12:2), mainly meant, and still means, "Stay away from the profane areas," ranging from politics to theaters.

The entire distinction between sacred and profane domains, as a horizontal distinction between structures, has to be utterly rejected. *Every* societal relationship, even politics and theaters, can become sacred if it is dedicated to God and his Kingdom. And *every* societal relationship, even churches and Bible clubs, can become profane if it—consciously or unconsciously—turns its back to God and his Kingdom. In principle, there are apostate and sacred families, apostate and sacred churches, apostate and sacred states, apostate and sacred schools, apostate and sacred companies, apostate and sacred cultural activities, apostate and sacred universities. I say "in principle," because too often we are dealing with some mixture of good and evil. No single earthly domain is totally wicked, and no single earthly domain is totally sacred and safe.

Far too often the path traveled by the Christ-believing pilgrim goes through very unsafe, wicked areas, with a few sacred rest areas along the way. But if his or her heart has been taken captive by God's Word and Spirit, it will spread light in any of the societal relationships, no matter how defectively.

Some might argue here that it cannot be true that any societal relationship or community as such could become sacred. They mention the example of a pack of thieves, or a brothel, or a church of Satan. Are these not societal relationships that as such are wicked? My answer is that this is the wrong question. A pack of thieves and a brothel are, according to their law structure, profit-making enterprises, and neither profit-making nor enterprises as such are wrong. However, at the subject side (see chapter 4 of my book *Wisdom for Thinkers* for these terms) we are dealing with an absolutely anti-normative realization of the entrepreneurial structure, in which the pack of thieves lives parasitically on the eighth ("You shall not steal"), and the brothel on the seventh commandment ("You shall not commit adultery," or more generally, "fornication") (Exod. 20:14-15).

Thus, the church of Satan, too, according to its law structure, is a church, in the sense of a religious community (if it is not instead a profit-making enterprise), and there is nothing wrong with respect to this law structure as such. However, with respect to the subject side, the church of Satan is the most anti-normative realization of a church structure one could imagine. It is an outright rebellion against the first commandment: "You shall have no other gods before [or, besides] me" (Exod. 20:3).

Heavenly Citizens

From the previous argument, we can now easily see how, in my opinion, the notions of pilgrimage and exile are to be understood, and how they can be linked with the notion of the Kingdom of God. Does the fact that we are foreigners, exiles, and pilgrims (1 Pet. 2:11) mean that we have nothing to do with earthly society? Longing for a heavenly country (Heb. 11:13-16)—does that imply that we do not want to have anything to do with our earthly country?

Not at all—and I can easily demonstrate that. Peter makes clear that our being foreigners does *not* imply that we have nothing to do with the earth anymore. On the contrary, he gives us several exhortations as to the earthly relationships or communities to which we certainly do belong: the state (vv. 13-17), work (vv. 18-25), marriage (3:1-7). Our pilgrimage and exile do not imply that we abstain from politics, from business, from marriage, but that we "abstain from sinful desires"! Not politics, not business, not marriage—the structures as such—are wrong, but all "sinful desires" in politics, business, and marriage. The structures are not wrong, but the apostate direction within these structures, or within individual life, is wrong. This reality applies to both non-believers and believers whose lives and drives are taken up with these structures. All who lose sight of the vertical dimension are forgetting their pilgrimage and fall prey to "sinful desires."

Likewise, the heavenly country in Hebrews 11 is not contrasted with the earthly country, as if we have nothing to do anymore with the latter. Abraham, Isaac, and Jacob were foreigners and pilgrims in Canaan, but they were very much involved with the affairs of the country in which they lived. We, too, participate in all kinds of earthly relationships, but our lives in them, and the tasks and responsibilities that we have within them, are governed by our longing for the heavenly country.

This may help us understand Philippians 3:20, "our citizenship is in heaven," that is, we are citizens of heaven; we possess a heavenly citizenship. Being foreigners as well as being citizens belong together as two sides of the same coin: foreigners here below, citizens there above. However, we *are* not yet there above. Our actual *position* is there, in Christ (Eph. 2:6), our actual life is there, hidden with Christ in God (Col. 3:3), but we *personally* are still on earth, with all concomitant offices, tasks, and responsibilities.

This earth, not heaven, is the very domain of the Kingdom of God. To be sure, in the Gospel according to Matthew, this kingdom is usually called the "Kingdom of heaven," but this is never intended to be a kingdom *in* heaven. Here the word heaven is nothing but a euphemism for "God" (cf. Luke 15:21, "sinned against heaven"; Matt. 5:34, "swearing by heaven"). The "Kingdom of heaven" is a kingdom in which "heaven," that is, Christ, reigns over the earth. Compare here what Daniel told Nebuchadnezzar, "Heaven rules," that is, the Most High God rules over the earth (Dan. 4:26). Living believers are citizens of a "heavenly" kingdom *on earth*.

The Christians' heavenly citizenship is not just something to look forward to, as something that will be realized at death, or at the second coming of Christ. Rather it is something to be realized here and now, in all societal relationships to which Christians belong. Christians have the calling to demonstrate in all earthly relationships the way that heavenly citizens behave in them. What kind of husbands and wives, parents and children, civil authorities and citizens, church leaders and church members, administrators, teachers and pupils, employers and employees, etc., are heavenly citizens? How do *heavenly* people behave in such *earthly* relationships? That way is different from that of the "earth-dwellers," that is, people who not only live on this earth, but who find their whole existence there, clinging to it because they have nothing else (cf. Rev. 3:10; 6:10; 8:13; 11:10; 13:8-14; 14:6).

What the apostle Paul says about believing slaves can basically be said of all believers: in the heavenly way they behave in all their earthly relationships and communities they "adorn the doctrine of our God and Savior in all things" (Titus 2:10 NKJV).

The Philippian Christians understood Paul's imagery very well because they lived in Philippi, which at that time had the status of a Roman colony. This meant that its inhabitants were considered to be citizens of Rome, although they lived in Philippi, far away from Rome. As citizens of Rome, the inhabitants were to take pride in showing to the whole Macedonian environment how a Roman citizen lives and works in Macedonia. Similarly, this earth is the "colony" where heavenly citizens are to show to their neighbors how a heavenly citizen lives and works on this earth.

We find parallel imagery in the epistles to the Ephesians and the Colossians. We saw that these epistles emphasize that our actual position, our actual life, exists in and with Christ in heaven. But this does not mean that these epistles encourage us to walk with our heads in the clouds. On the contrary, in the second half of both epistles, our feet are given firm footing on the ground by showing us how a heavenly citizen glorifies God, and serves his neighbor, in such very earthly relationships as the local congregation, marriage, family, and work (Eph. 4:17–6:9; Col. 3:9–4:1). Therefore, the Christian is not only a heavenly citizen, but also a citizen of the Kingdom of God, and that is on earth. (I even wonder if these two things are not basically the same.) The believer enjoys his position in the heavenly realms in Christ (Eph. 2:6), but he also possesses his "inheritance in the kingdom of Christ and God" (5:5). The believer's life is "hidden with Christ in God" (Col. 3:3), but he has also been "transferred . . . to the kingdom of his [i.e., the Father's] beloved Son" (1:13), and has been made a fellow worker for the Kingdom of God (cf. 4:11).

True Life

Heavenly citizens on earth—where do we put the emphasis, on *heavenly*, or on *earth*? We may argue that, although we are heavenly citizens, this has to be made visible in our earthly relationships. Then the emphasis is on our earthly functioning. We could also argue that, although we have all kinds of earthly offices and responsibilities, we should not lose sight of the vertical dimension: our *true life* lies with Christ in God. If we put the emphasis this way, there is less chance that we will consider the earth as an "enduring city" (Heb. 13:14). We are looking for "the city that is to come." We are foreigners and pilgrims like Abraham, who (negatively) did not only feel foreign toward his surroundings, but (positively) was looking forward to the "city with foundations, whose architect and builder is God" (Heb. 11:10). Remember: for every foreigner there is one place where he is *no* foreigner: *home*.

Faith always has these two dimensions, the anticipative one—looking forward—and the vertical one—looking up. You find both in Hebrews 11:1. Faith is "the assurance of things hoped for," as we see demonstrated in the patriarchs: they looked forward to what God had prepared for them, and would one day give them. But faith is also the "the conviction of things not seen." That is, being a foreigner involves not only pilgrimage, that is, being "on the way" to the city that is to come, but also "seeing him who is invisible" (v. 27), that is, *right now*. Faith is a fellowship with God *now*, a life hidden with Christ in God *now*, the "friendship" of the Lord for "those who fear him" *now* (Ps. 25:14).

For the believer, there is always more—already now—than all earthly offices and responsibilities together. The New Testament never speaks negatively of earthly things as such. On the contrary, "everything created by God is good, and nothing is to be rejected if it is received with thanksgiving, for it is made holy by the word of God and prayer" (1 Tim. 4:4-5). But what the New Testament does warn against is *being preoccupied* with the earthly things (cf. Phil. 3:19), so that the vertical dimension gets lost. "If then you have been raised with Christ, seek the things that are above, where Christ is, seated at the right hand of God. Set your minds on things that are above, not on *things that are on earth*" (Col. 3:1-2; italics added). "For many . . . walk as enemies of the cross of Christ. Their end is destruction, their god is their belly, and they glory in their shame, with minds set on *earthly things*" (Phil. 3:18-19; italics added). After this, we find in Colossians 3 and Philippians 3 the verses already quoted.

This upward dimension is that which the King explained to his disciples in the Sermon of the Mount: "Do not lay up for yourselves treasures on earth, where moth and rust destroy and where thieves break in and steal, but lay up for yourselves treasures in heaven, where neither moth nor rust destroys and where thieves do not break in and steal. For where your treasure is, there your heart will be also" (Matt. 6:19-21). And just before he appeared to three of his disciples in royal glory—as a picture of the Kingdom to come (Matt. 17)—he said, "If anyone would come after me, let him deny himself and take up his cross and follow me. For whoever would save his life will lose it, but whoever loses his life for my sake will find it. For what will it profit a man if he gains the whole world and forfeits his soul? Or what shall a man give in return for his soul? For the Son of Man is going to come with his angels in the glory of his Father, and then he will repay each person according to what he has done" (16:24-27).

In 1 Timothy 6, Paul addresses his reproaches, not to those who are rich but to those who *want* to be rich, for they "fall into temptation, into a snare, into many senseless and harmful desires that plunge people into ruin and destruction" (v. 9). To "the rich in this present age" the warning comes "not to be haughty, nor to set their hopes on the uncertainty of riches, but on God, who richly provides us with everything [including earthly wealth, wjo] to enjoy." But then, too, to charge them "to do good, to be rich in good works, to be generous and ready to share, thus storing up treasure for themselves as a good foundation for the future, so that they may take hold of *that which is truly life*" (vv. 17-19).

This is what matters: not to "store up things for ourselves" but to be "rich toward God" (Luke 12:21 NIV). This leads us back to the Kingdom of God because the latter text continues: "[D]o not be anxious about your life, what you will eat, nor about your body, what you will put on [the earthly things, wjo] . . . [D]o not seek what you are to eat and what you are to drink, nor be worried. For all the nations of the world seek after these things, and your Father knows that you need them. Instead, seek his kingdom, and these things will be added to you" (vv. 22, 29-31). *First things first!*

Suffering

Everyone who, as a foreigner, as a pilgrim, as a heavenly citizen, as one who sets his mind on things above, functions this way in all earthly relationships in which he has been placed, will experience suffering. These are the effect of the constant tension between the believer's heavenly citizenship and his earthly affairs. In the present age, the Kingdom of God realizes itself in a world that is still pervaded with sin, death, and Satan. As a consequence, every disciple of the Kingdom will have to expect the "reproach of Christ" (Heb. 11:26). Therefore, right at the beginning of his so-called "Constitution of the Kingdom," the Master says, "Blessed are those who are persecuted for righteousness' sake, for theirs is the kingdom of heaven. Blessed are you when others revile you and persecute you and utter all kinds of evil against you falsely on my account. Rejoice and be glad, for your reward is great in heaven" (Matt. 5:10-12).

Elsewhere, Jesus told his disciples, "If the world hates you, know that it has hated me before it hated you. If you were of the world, the world would love you as its own; but because you are not of the world, but I chose you out of the world, therefore the world hates you. Remember the word that I said to you: 'A servant is not greater than his master' (John 13:16). If they persecuted me, they will also persecute you" (John 15:18-20). Paul and Barnabas told the disciples in Antioch, "[T]hrough many tribulations we must enter the kingdom of God" (Acts 14:22).

Discipleship means suffering. As long as Satan is still the god and prince of this world, much Christian work in the Kingdom of God will involve suffering for the believer. For parents and children suffer under each other's shortcomings, and sometimes even under each other's wickedness. The same holds for husbands and wives, teachers and pupils, employers and employees, elders and common church members, authorities and common citizens. In all these relationships people can truly terrorize one another. Those who hold certain offices suffer under the rebellion and disobedience of those who should respect them. The latter suffer under the misfeasance and brutality of persons in authority. Suffering often means taking the lowest place, "like men sentenced to death, because we have become a spectacle to the world, to angels, and to men" (1 Cor. 4:9).

This does not mean that the Christian always necessarily takes the lowest position *in society*. To claim such a thing would again mean a typical confusion of structure and direction. Whoever forgets his Christian calling, reigns as a "king" without bothering about God or his commandments (v. 8), whether he is a prime minister or a laborer. But he who really fulfills his Christian calling, will necessarily suffer in a sinful world, whether he is a prime minister or a laborer. The laborer in the voting booth, who in a humanist way confuses his right to vote with the right to rule, behaves as a king. The prime minister who knows his calling to stand under God's dominion behaves as a servant. (We remember that the word "minister" literally does mean "servant"; it is a relic from the time when the government minister still was the servant of an absolute monarch "by the grace of God," and thus indirectly a servant of God.)

The Mind of Christ

Discipleship does not necessarily imply taking the lowest place in society, as if believing chief executive officers, university presidents, and magistrates were to be condemned for their high societal positions. Discipleship does mean taking the lowest place *spiritually*: the place of the reproach of Christ. Paul's commandment, "Do not be haughty, but associate with the lowly" (Rom. 12:16), is *not* an appeal to take the lowest position in social life but the appeal, whatever position one has, low or high, to function in that position in a spirit of simplicity, humility, meekness, in brief: in the spirit of Christ.

This, I presume, is one of the reasons why Jesus told his disciples, "Truly, I say to you, unless you turn and become like children, you will never enter the kingdom of heaven. Whoever humbles himself like this child is the greatest in the kingdom of heaven" (Matt. 18:3-4). Believers are not to imitate the childishness of the child—on the contrary, in that sense they have to grow up (e.g., 1 Cor. 3:1-3; 14:20; Eph. 4:14; Heb. 5:12-14)—but the simplicity of the child, his being without airs, without a self-made pedestal from which he could fall.

Here again, the King is the great example for every disciple in the Kingdom of God. He took the lowest place. "Learn from me, for I am gentle and lowly in heart" (Matt. 11:29). But this did not mean that he gave up his high status! There was no false modesty with him: "You call me Teacher and Lord, and you are right, for so I am" (John 13:13). Nothing could be taken away from this. Taking the lowest place did not mean that he ever stopped to be the Master and Lord. What *did* it mean, then? Listen to what he adds immediately, "If I then, your Lord and Teacher, have washed your feet, you also ought to wash one another's feet. For I have given you an example, that you also should do just as I have done to you" (vv. 14-15). Christ did not take the lowest place hierarchically, but spiritually, in that he, without stopping to be their Master, bowed down to wash the feet of his disciples (also cf. Matt. 23:8-12; Luke 22:24-30).

Political offices belong to the highest offices that a nation knows. But status is something very different from the attitude with which political offices, or any offices, are conducted. The believing, simple, humble, modest magistrate is a servant and follower of the great King, but he does not stop being a magistrate. His office is high, but his attitude is humble. Humility does not exclude authority, and authority does not exclude humility. Every husband, parent, elder, bishop, magistrate, director, chairman, and president must be humble, and give him- or herself away in servitude to their subordinates. But that does not take anything away from the status of his or her office. The lowest office can be fulfilled in pride and arrogance, and the highest office can be carried out in humility and servitude. (The reverse is also true, of course.) I repeat, the status of the office and the attitude of the official are two very different matters. The highest Office-bearer this earth has ever seen was the humblest of all.

Questions for Review

1. What are the two meanings of the word *world*, as we find them in the Bible?

2. Why is no societal relationship evil in itself?

3. Why must we reject the distinction between the *sacred* and the *profane*?

4. Using the analogy of a Roman colony (like Philippi), explain what it means that we are *heavenly citizens here on earth*.

5. Why is it a false dilemma to choose between our "life in heaven" and our "life on earth"?

6. Why will living on earth like citizens of heaven inevitably bring about suffering for Christians?

7. How is it possible to occupy a high position in society, and yet do so with humility?

Chapter Six

THE TWO KINGDOMS

Several times in the previous chapters, I referred to the relationship between church and state. I did this particularly in chapter 3, where we saw that the notion of distinct offices and responsibilities forbids placing the church under the state, as well as placing the state under the church. In chapter 4, I mentioned the problem of ecclesiocracy: a political form in which all societal relationships, including the state, are made subservient to the church. If indeed, among all the various societal relationships, there are two that are particularly likely to be placed above all the others, in church history these have traditionally been the church and the state.

Scholastic Background

In Christian thinking, since the Christianization of the Roman empire (fourth century), time and again the question has arisen: Is God's government to be associated primarily with the church, or primarily with the state? And if perhaps with both, which of the two has the primacy? In the fourth century, after the Christianization of the Roman empire, the answer was *caesaropapism:* the Roman emperor practically functioned as the leader of the Christian commonwealth. For instance, it was he who convened and formally presided the Council of Nicea (325).

In the thirteenth century, it was the other way around: pope Innocent III not only enjoyed supremacy in the church, but also in the Western world. In those days, it was said that not only the bishops, but also the Holy Roman emperor and the kings of the various Western countries, could not so much as lift their little finger without the pope's permission.

It is quite understandable that both situations occurred—at different times, of course—because it seems that "convincing" arguments can be adduced for both viewpoints. If we put the emphasis on the spiritual character of the Kingdom of God, we will give the primacy to the church, for the church is spiritual (sacred), and the state is worldly (profane, secular). However, if we put the emphasis on God's government over the whole of humanity, we will give the primacy to the state. And if people refuse to choose between the pope and the emperor, they will construe some kind of *duplex ordo* ("double order"). This is a scheme in which the two, church and state, are put next to each other as two different "realms" or "regiments" (that is, "regimes") of equal value. They are considered to be two facets of God's government. You will most often hear these identified as "two kingdoms," so this is the terminology we will use as well.

The terminology I just introduced may be a little misleading. "Realms" and "regiments" are not the same. If we speak of two "realms," or "empires," or "kingdoms," we might think that the reference is to the Kingdom of God and the kingdom of Satan. However, the term "regiment" has a very different meaning. It is meant to express the idea that both in the church and in the state we are dealing with a divine regime, rule of government. With the former regime, the church, also called the regime of the "gospel," God leads people to faith. With the other regime, the state, also called the regime of the "law," God keeps a check on the unrighteous. In the former kingdom we have to do with the *iustitia fidei*, "the justice (or, righteousness) of faith" (cf. Rom. 4:11,13). In the latter kingdom we have to do with the *iustitia civilis* or *politica*, the "civil (or, political) justice (or, righteousness)," that is, the outward righteousness of societal life.

In the light of the previous chapters, it may have become clear why I fundamentally reject this whole question about the primacy of church or state *a priori*. However, the doctrine of the two kingdoms, which appears in many different forms, has been so influential that we must look at it a little more closely. That will also give us the opportunity to search for the deeper roots of this doctrine. These roots are to be found in scholasticism, that is, the philosophy of medieval Christian thinkers who accepted the dualism of *nature* and *grace*, a dualism that, in later humanism, was secularized into the dualism of *nature* and *freedom*.

Scholastic thought, as it has been formulated especially by Thomas Aquinas (thirteenth century), is characterized by the all-encompassing dualism of grace and nature. This manifests itself in numerous well-known other dualisms: church and world, soul and body (in the ancient Greek sense of the soul and body "substance"), heaven and earth, the sacred and the secular, that which is Christian versus that which is human, faith and reason, sacred theology and profane philosophy (including the special sciences), supernatural and natural theology, special and general revelation, faith experience and faith knowledge, "heart and head," etc.

Even if, in modern theology, some of these forms of the Nature–Grace dualism are not fashionable anymore, the same dualism nevertheless lives on in a very vital way, under various names and in various forms. These forms may look very different, but they amount to the same basic dualism. In all these cases, a domain of divine, sacred activity is distinguished from a kind of neutral (secular, profane) domain. In the latter domain, human reason is considered to be more or less autonomous, so that it is able to function according to its light. In the sacred domain, however, reason does not function by its own light but by that of Scripture and faith. All these false dualisms have something in common that I could briefly summarize as the *curse of neutrality*. We will come back to this vital subject several times.

Types of Two-Kingdoms Doctrine

According to the Nature–Grace scheme, scholastic dualism identifies two "realms," "regiments," or "kingdoms" which are clearly distinguished, thought to be fundamentally irreducible to each other, and independent of one another. This corresponds with the well-known Lutheran dualism of *law and gospel*: the law is the norm for the former, the gospel is the norm for the latter kingdom. In Lutheran terminology, they are the kingdom of God's left and the realm of his right hand, respectively. The one domain is that of nature: the domain of temporal, earthly, natural, rational, secular, profane life, which also includes the state. The other domain is that of grace: the domain of the eternal, spiritual, supernatural, pistical, divine, sacred life, which also includes the church.

Please note: the former domain, that of the state, is not at all viewed as separated from God, for the authority of the worldly kings and presidents is also God-given authority (Rom. 13:1-7; 1 Pet. 2:13-17). In this respect, this domain, too, is a divine "realm" or "regiment," in which God realizes certain purposes, namely, maintaining order and peace in temporal, earthly life, and constraining the unrighteous. Yet, this realm is thought to be far removed from the actual Kingdom of God, the spiritual Kingdom of his Christ, which realizes itself within the church.

Thus, the most striking characteristic of whatever type of two-kingdoms doctrine we may encounter is always the secularization of the state. Sacred (spiritual) life, the life of faith, is found in the church, as well as in the personal, inner life of faith. For the rest, the entire life of the believer is secularized, or considered to be neutral, as people often put it. According to this scheme of thinking, apart from church life and the inner life of faith, the Christian's life is just as secularized as that of non-Christians. Professional life, science, schooling, business, the arts, politics, etc. are considered to be neutral. Some advocates of this view who deny that they are defending neutrality nevertheless see no place for faith affecting *societal relationships and structures*, but have room only for faith-directed *personal, individual relationships* in the world. A Christian state is viewed as a fundamental impossibility, and at best, Christian schools are tolerated as long as they are entirely financed by the parents. Here, again, a Christian school is understood in terms of individual Christians providing education that is, with the exception of a Bible class, just as secular and neutral as that of the state schools. People committed to this view often assert, for example, that there is no such thing as "Christian mathematics." So then, only the church is thought to represent the Kingdom of God on earth: the state can at best serve the Kingdom of God by helping, supporting, and defending the church.

Some years ago, in an African country, I heard a well-known African theologian defend the two-kingdoms doctrine in such strong terms that he even rejected the *principle* of a Christian state. He explained that, in a certain African country, where more than 90% of the people confess the Christian faith, he had pleaded very strongly with the government *not* to establish, under any circumstances, a Christian state! To him, a Christian state necessarily seemed to imply the suppression of the non-Christians within that state. Therefore, the state definitely had to be neutral! This is what happens when you leave philosophy and politicology to the theologians, even Bible-believing theologians. They may think they can adduce biblical arguments, but in reality they are caught in the age-old two-kingdoms doctrine.

This African theologian, though with the best of intentions, had not even grasped the notion of a state that has *no other* task than maintaining public justice, without interfering with the beliefs of individual persons. In this sense, the Christian state will never enforce Christian beliefs on its citizens. Apparently, my African colleague could think of the Christian state as being only a totalitarian state.

One practical example: a Christian government does not prohibit the building of mosques by Muslims. This is not because this government is pro-Islam—it is not—but because it does not meddle in the religious convictions of its citizens. A Christian government must guarantee to all people the same religious freedom that Christians would like to enjoy in all countries of the world. Please note again: this has nothing to do with the state being neutral. It never is. The authorities always have their own personal beliefs; they may be pro- or anti-Christian, pro- or anti-Islam. That is not the point. The point is that the power of any government ought never to go any further than to maintain public justice. Therefore, the state has a say about the external conditions under which mosques (synagogues, temples) are built, not with this building as such.

Creation and Re-Creation

In the next chapter, I will describe the Nature–Grace dualism in terms of a dualism of creation and re-creation. The natural realm of the earthly and human realities is thought to belong to the first creation, and the supernatural (spiritual) realm of the Kingdom of God in Christ is associated with the coming re-creation. The two are dialectically placed over against one another. The Kingdom of God is no longer seen as a realm that realizes itself within *this* creation. The reason is that people do not see that God is not going to *replace* the old creation but to *elevate* it through redemption. If it were otherwise, in a certain sense Satan would have gained a victory: he would have corrupted the old creation to such an extent that the only thing God can do is to replace it by another, new creation. But that is not the case at all. I argue that it is *this* creation that God wants to restore and renew. However, the two-kingdoms doctrine argues that in the church, as (the germ of) the Kingdom of God, the beginning of the re-creation is to be seen, which is supposed to stand dialectically over against the old creation. In this view, the state, as we know it today, is only a temporary arrangement by God to create and maintain order among humans until the last day, that is, as long as the old creation still continues.

In regard to the relationship between church and state, of course a lot of varieties may be, and have been, invented. For instance, it makes a lot of difference whether one sees the state particularly as the domain of Satan, or whether one considers it to be a "realm" ("regiment") of God, albeit one that is sharply distinguished from the Kingdom of God. The most drastic separation between church and state occurs there where religion is repulsed from public life altogether. Here we are no longer dealing with just a separation of church and state, but a separation of religion and society, which, as I have argued before, are very different matters. In such a situation, the illusion of the neutral state—and in its wake, the illusion of the neutral school—is defended and implemented most strongly. I repeat that I do believe in the separation between church and state—but a separation between religion and society is not only undesirable, but impossible: *religion (including ideologies) is everywhere.*

In the Lutheran view of the state, we find a similar separation between church and state as in the traditional view, but it is less strong. It is true, as the spiritual and the temporal realms, respectively, church and state have no inner connection, according to this view. However, the state is not neutral but sacred, for the king, prince, duke, or count receives his authority from God, and is responsible to him, not to the church. At best, there is a relationship with the church to the extent that the church, besides being a spiritual realm, is an earthly institution as well, which as such falls under the jurisdiction of the state. However, the state does not meddle in church affairs, just as the church does not meddle in state affairs.

The consequences of Luther's views in sixteenth-century Germany are well known. On behalf of the freshly started "Evangelical" (Protestant) church, Luther sought the support of the German princes who had become Protestants. He vehemently opposed the very poor German peasants in the Peasant's War (1524-1526), because in his opinion the peasants' rebellion was outright rebellion against God. At the Peace of Augsburg (1555, after Luther's death), Catholics and Lutherans agreed on the famous slogan, *Cuius regio, eius religio*, "Whose realm, his religion" (the phrase itself was coined in 1582). That is, the religion of the prince dictates the religion of his subjects, either Catholic or Lutheran. The principle did not hold for Calvinist (Reformed) princes, and for Anabaptist regions. Inhabitants who could not conform to their prince's religion were allowed to leave his realm.

Other Varieties

In the following three views, we see a closer relationship between church and state, although still understood in terms of the Nature–Grace dualism. In these views, the state allegedly has the God-given task of helping, supporting, and defending the church. In the medieval Roman Catholic view of the state, the state renders this service from a lower position than the church. That is, when interests conflict or overlap, the church stands above the state. It is also the church that determines what are the spiritual interests that the state must defend. Think of the Inquisition, a church organization that hunted, tried, and condemned heretics, and then handed them over to the state, which then executed them. In this respect, the state was entirely subservient to the church. However, usually the church did not meddle in common, secular state affairs.

In the Anglican or Episcopalian church, too, the state must support the church, but in this case, the state does so from a higher position than the church. This is because the church in its earthly manifestation is considered to be a part of the all-encompassing state. Therefore, the British monarch is also head of the Church of England, and *Fidei defensor,* "defender of the faith." Even today, the British queen is officially called "Elizabeth the Second, by the Grace of God, of the United Kingdom of Great Britain and Northern Ireland and of Her other Realms and Territories Queen, Head of the Commonwealth, Defender of the Faith." Within the British Commonwealth, the addition, "Defender of the Faith," is retained only in Canada and New Zealand, although these countries have no state churches. Here, the sovereign is seen as a defender of faith in the most general sense.

In the Anglican view, the church always submits to the state in the case of conflicting or overlapping interests. It is the state that rules over secular as well as sacred affairs, that is, also over the internal functioning of the church, for instance, when it comes to appointing (arch)bishops. The choice of a new archbishop of Canterbury, who is the principal leader of the Church of England, is announced by the British prime minister in the name of the Sovereign. However, the state does not meddle in the strictly spiritual tasks of the church, such as preaching the Word and administering the sacraments.

Also in the classical Reformed view of the state, as formulated by John Calvin and as applied particularly in the Netherlands (sixteenth—nineteenth centuries), the state was supposed to support the church with the purpose of furthering the Kingdom of God. This task traditionally included combating false religions and false churches and sects (see the unrevised Article 36 of the Belgic Confession; cf. chapter 4 above). Since it is the spiritual Kingdom of Christ, the church is higher than the state, but this does not imply that it can exert any authority over the state. On the contrary, as we said before, in the seventeenth century, it was not the church leaders but the States-General that convened the well known Synod of Dort (1618-1619). This was seen as part of maintaining public justice: there was a serious theological conflict going on in the church, between the so-called Remonstrants and the Contra-Remonstrants, which caused great upheaval in society. Seldom did a theological issue touch the general public to such an extent. Therefore, the States-General saw it as its duty to convene the church leaders to solve the problems that had arisen and thus restore tranquility and peace in society. In this respect, however, the state had neither a higher position than the church, as in the Anglican view, nor a lower position, as in the traditional Roman Catholic view, but an equal position. This meant that both church and state were viewed as standing under the authority of Scripture, and as both being responsible to God alone.

An Alternate Route

Scholastic thinking, which underlies especially the Roman Catholic variety of the two-kingdoms doctrine, is totally at variance with the great Reformational discovery of, first, the radicality of *creation*. That is, creation is entirely, and at its *radix* (i.e., root), dependent upon God, and designed for service and honor to him. Secondly, the view being referred to is at variance with the radicality of the *fall* of Man. Through this fall, Man in his entirety, including his reason, and consequently also the cosmos as a whole, was corrupted by sin. Thirdly, the view under consideration is at variance with the radicality of *redemption*, through which repentant Man as a whole, as well as *all* his temporal relationships, is redeemed from the power of sin and Satan. Fourthly, the view is at variance with the *eschaton* (the "end of the ages," 1 Cor. 10:11; Heb. 9:26), in which all creation will be restored to communion with, and the glorification of, God.

This important Reformational discovery of a threefold radicality implies the utter rejection of any notion of neutral domains, as well as a view in which all of human life either as corrupted by sin, or as restored to the service of God. By the way, unfortunately, this important Reformational discovery has never really conquered all the areas of Reformational thinking. On the contrary, the scholastic Nature–Grace scheme pops up at many places in Reformational theology (see my forthcoming *Introduction to Christian Theology*), as well as in the Reformational doctrine of the state.

Perhaps those views of the state that place the church under the state, as in the Lutheran and the Anglican, as well as the original Reformed views, do not seem to be rooted in scholastic thinking. This is because, according to scholasticism, the church, as being under Grace, is allegedly *higher* than the state, which falls within Nature. However, there is only a seeming discrepancy here. In the views mentioned, the church stands under the state only insofar as it is an earthly societal relationship. In its character as the spiritual kingdom of God it necessarily *does* stand higher than the state, which is only the earthly, temporal kingdom of God. Therefore, also in the Lutheran and the Anglican, as well as the original Reformed views of the state, the state is never to meddle in the actual, ecclesial matters of preaching the Word and administering the sacraments.

In this respect, even the Lutheran, Anglican, and early Reformed views of the state are still strongly rooted in the scholastic Nature–Grace scheme. There is an important difference, though: the great *gain* of the Reformation was that both Martin Luther and John Calvin did not view church and state primarily in their mutual relationship, but as being both subjected to the Word of God. In this respect, tremendous progress was made: they no longer distinguished between a neutral and a sacred domain; on the contrary, in their (biblical) view, *all* domains are subjected to God. To Christ has been given dominion over *all* things, not just sacred things. In this sense, the dualism of sacred and secular is to be entirely rejected. Actually, many Bible believing Roman Catholic friends today would in practice confess the same truth: Christ's kingship covers all domains of life and society.

In this context, people have often quoted the famous words of Abraham Kuyper (1880, in his lecture at the opening of his Free University in Amsterdam), "There is not a square inch in the whole domain of our human existence over which Christ, who is Sovereign over all, does not cry: 'Mine!'"

An Essentially New Approach

What early Lutheran, early Anglican, and early Reformed thinking—as well as Catholic thinking, for that matter—badly needed was an entirely new Christian view of cosmic reality, in which the power of traditional Nature–Grace thinking would be fundamentally broken. I already discussed some elements of such a new way of thinking, such as the plurality of offices and responsibilities (chapter 3), the notion of theocracy (chapter 4), and the elements of structure and direction (chapters 3-5).

It is of the utmost importance to distinguish between the medieval and early-Protestant Nature–Grace dualism, and the new Christian view of the state. In scholastic dualism, the directional antitheses between God and Satan, or between the Spirit and the flesh (cf. Gal. 5:16-18), are replaced by an alleged antithesis that, so to say, is perpendicular to the one just mentioned: an artificial structural antithesis within created reality, namely, between church and state. In such a view, the Kingdom of God is supposedly realized through the church, and in spite of, *or* with the help of, the allegedly neutral state. In reality, the directional antithesis between Spirit and flesh runs right through what is allegedly natural, such as the state, as well as what is allegedly supernatural, such as the church. That is, it runs right through the two realms or kingdoms. In other words, this antithesis of God and Satan, of Spirit and flesh, manifests itself both in the church and in the state, and likewise in every other societal relationship: within both the "sacred" and the "secular" domains, within both the domain of faith and that of reason (if we may still use these misleading distinctions for the sake of the argument).

In his *De civitate Dei*, "The City of God" (written between 413 and 426), the great church father Augustine discerned very well that the *civitas Dei*, the commonwealth (or city) of God—let us say, the Kingdom of God—cannot simply be equated with the church, and the *civitas terrena*, the earthly realm (in which both good and evil powers are at work), cannot simply be equated with the state. Of course not; in Augustine's time there were Christian (or "Christian") emperors on the thrones of Rome and Constantinople! In Augustine's view, there was also something of the *civitas Dei* in the state, and something of the *civitas terrena* in the church. But in the end, Augustine, too, erroneously associated the directional antithesis of the two *civitates,* particularly with the structural antithesis between church and state.

In my opinion, the terms *civitas Dei* and *civitas terrena* as such are quite appropriate, but only if they are used as a *directional* antithesis. This antithesis manifests itself equally in every societal relationship, both within the church and within the state, as well as within marriage, the family, the school, the company, the party, the association, etc. Instead of this, unfortunately, the two terms have been abused time and again to draw a dividing-line within created reality—between church and state—thus blurring the distinction between structure and direction.

The Subsidiarity Principle

It is significant to see that in the Roman Catholic notion of "subsidiarity," exactly the same distinction between structure and direction is at stake. The principle of subsidiarity views the various societal relationships in a strongly hierarchical way. It is founded in the medieval notion of the *corpus Christianum*, the whole of all Christendom. This *corpus* is seen as the Christianized society, which is an organic and hierarchical entity constructed of several layers. That is, the lower layers, such as the family, the school, the company, are viewed as autonomous, independent, but yet *parts* of the state. This implies that the state can intervene in cases where the lower communities themselves are not able to fulfill their task of serving the greater whole, namely, the state.

In this way, there is a natural relationship between the Catholic subsidiarity doctrine and the social-democratic view of the state. In both cases, the role of the state tends to become too dominating: the state is apt to easily assume tasks that actually do not belong to itself but to other societal relationships. Take, for instance, the school: if the school is seen as part of the state, the state can easily find excuses to take over (part of) its tasks. However, if the school is a societal relationship distinct from, and on equal footing with, the state, then the state may never meddle in the internal affairs of the school. It may only create the pre-conditions of schools as a matter of public justice, as explained before. *The state does not teach.* Only teachers do that, not on behalf of the state, but on behalf of the parents.

In the subsidiarity doctrine, all the emphasis is laid on *structure*: there is one structure, one society, with—apart from the church—the state at the top, and family, school, company, association, party, etc. belonging to the lower layers. The (God-ward) direction runs from the church through the state to the lower levels. In the sphere sovereignty doctrine, however, there are no layers but only societal relationships that all stand on an equal level and all exhibit a God-ward or an apostate direction, or a mixture of the two. This *direction* of every societal relationship *never* runs via either the church or the state, but is always a matter of direct responsibility to God.

Certainly as a consequence of secularization, the subsidiarity principle, though well intended at the outset, has more and more become a pragmatic principle. For instance, if it is more practical that the state should organize the schools within its territory, instead of private educational organizations doing this, let the state do so. This is why Roman Catholic thinking is always rather defenseless when the state threatens to disallow Christian schools within its boundaries. On the basis of the (secularized) subsidiarity principle, the "freedom of education"—all religions and ideologies having the freedom to establish their own schools, if they like—could easily be viewed as an impractical, inefficient use of taxpayers' money, and thus be surrendered.

Roman Catholics would have a much stronger case if they too would accept the principle of sphere sovereignty, or, if you like, the notion of the plurality of offices and responsibilities (see chapter 3). It is *not* the responsibility of the state to organize all schooling, for the simple reason that schools are extensions of the families, not of the state. It is *parents* who organize schools through the educational organizations they establish, or through existing Christian organizations. It is the *state* that has to maintain public justice, and nothing else; that is, (a) to facilitate the construction of school buildings, (b) to check the quality of the education offered in these schools (inspection), and (c) to supply schools only for those children whose parents do not care about having their own schools. *That is all.* Everything that goes beyond this will land us in the arms of the socialists, who would like to see the state encompass all the other societal relationships, and sacrifice the latter's own responsibilities.

The task of the state is to maintain public justice, nothing more and nothing less. Socialists always want to *expand* this task, and include in it responsibilities that actually belong to other societal relationships. Libertarians always want to *restrict* this task, and hand over some of the state's own responsibilities to private organizations. This is why Christian politics always has to fight on two fronts, and always has to define anew the proper route between the two, on the basis of an elaborate Christian doctrine of the state.

Creation and the Kingdom of God are not two structurally different realms (see the next chapters). Apostate creation and redeemed creation are structurally one and the same creation—with a diametrically opposed direction, however. The Kingdom of God sets out to manifest itself in every societal relationship, in every area of human life, in every cultural domain, when and where such a relationship or domain is no longer sin- and Satan-oriented, but God- and Christ-oriented, at least in principle. There is not the slightest room here for a dualism of law and gospel: both God's creational Word (law) and his redemptive Word (gospel) are contained in the eternal Torah. Both the first creation and the redeemed creation are subject to the same eternal Torah, as embodied in Christ.

Questions for Review

1. How does the two-kingdoms doctrine relate to the Nature–Grace dualism?

2. Why do some thinkers object to establishing a Christian state? What response to this objection does this chapter provide?

3. "God is not going to *replace* the old creation but to *elevate* it through redemption." What implications does this truth have for evaluating the two-kingdoms doctrine?

4. How does a biblical view of the Kingdom of God protect religious freedom for all citizens in a country?

5. Explain, in terms of the distinction between *structure* and *direction*, the Reformational view of creation, fall, and redemption.

6. Why is it mistaken to see Augustine's teaching about the city of God and the city of man as equivalent to two kingdoms?

7. Why is the teaching of sphere sovereignty preferable to the teaching of subsidiarity?

Chapter Seven
CREATION AND RE-CREATION

In the previous chapters I have dealt with some vital aspects in regard to the Kingdom of God, on the one hand, and the societal relationships or communities, on the other. When we speak about the Kingdom of God, we have a great perspective in front of us: the "age to come" (Mark 10:30; Eph. 1:21; Heb. 6:5) and the "world to come" (Heb. 2:5), a world of peace and righteousness, when the knowledge of God's glory will fill the earth (Isa. 11:9; Hab. 2:14). When we think of the societal relationships, we have as the foundation beneath our feet the creational ordinances of God, that is, the law-order that he has instituted for cosmic reality. These creational ordinances belong to the perspective of creation; the "world to come" belongs to the perspective of re-creation.

I am convinced that we need *both* perspectives in order to get a full and balanced picture of society: what is its creational foundation, and what is the eschatological future that God has prepared for it?

The Gospel of the Kingdom

Some people, especially those of a so-called Evangelical background, do not like such a double approach very much. Speaking about creational ordinances and law-order is too abstract for them, perhaps even legalistic. They would like to see the *gospel of Jesus Christ* occupy the central place in our Christian view of society and the state. Or, what is worse, they seldom seem to be interested in society, in the state, in culture, in science, at all. They seem to be interested only in the salvation of souls (James 1:21; 1 Pet. 1:9, 22; cf. Matt. 11:29; 2 Cor. 12:15).

In a sense, I can agree with all those who want to place the gospel at the center of all Christian thinking. But what precisely does this involve? Do many Bible-believing Christians not have a very narrow idea of the content and extent of "the gospel"?

In Luke 24:47, the risen Lord announces that "repentance and forgiveness of sins should be proclaimed in his [i.e., Messiah's] name to all nations." That is a well-known, very familiar description of the gospel: it is about sin, repentance, forgiveness, and salvation. If you would ask the average Bible-believing Christian to summarize "the" gospel in just a few words, you would very probably hear words like sin, atonement through the cross of Jesus, forgiveness, eternal salvation. As a Reformed theologian once asked me on a radio program, "Do you not agree with me, Willem, that the whole gospel can be summarized in two words, 'sin' and 'grace'?" I felt very sorry for him that I had to answer, "No, unfortunately I cannot agree."

Now, please understand me well! We certainly should keep preaching the gospel of forgiveness for poor sinners by the grace of God, on the basis of the redemptive work of Christ. It is an important and beautiful gospel. But it is not the full gospel! I do not mean this at all in the one-sided sense that Full Gospel Churches have given to this phrase. No, I am referring to what Jesus said in his Sermon on the Last Things (Matt. 24:14): "This *gospel of the kingdom* will be proclaimed throughout the whole world as a testimony to all nations, and then the end will come," that is, the end of the present age, at the second coming of Jesus (v. 3). Here, Jesus is referring to the "gospel of the Kingdom" that was going to be preached to all nations. How many Bible-believing Christians could easily give a brief summary of *this* (part of the) gospel? They want the gospel to occupy the central place in our view of society, the state, and politics. Fine. But then, let it be the gospel of the Kingdom.

At the end of the Gospel according to Matthew, Jesus himself gave a brief summary of this very gospel (without any reference to sin, atonement, and forgiveness—*that* reference was reserved for Luke 24): "All authority in heaven and on earth has been given to me. Go therefore and make disciples of all nations, baptizing them in the name of the Father and of the Son and of the Holy Spirit, teaching them to observe all that I have commanded you" (Matt. 28:18-20). In brief: I am the King of the heavens and the earth. *Therefore*—that is, in the light of this overwhelming and all-encompassing fact—go out everywhere, and challenge all people worldwide to take sides with *that* King, over against the kingdom of Satan. Invite people to become followers of this new King. They become this through baptism (by which the followers-to-be symbolically move from the one kingdom to the other), and subsequently through teaching.

This is a vital point. *What* is going to be taught in the Kingdom, on the "other side" of baptism? We could think of all kinds of lessons that are to be taught to young followers of Jesus, but notice what Jesus says here: "teaching them to *obey all that I have commanded you.*" Teach these young Christians my commands! That is why Christian parents are to bring their children up "in the discipline and instruction of the Lord" (Eph. 6:4). Notice, not just Jesus, but *the Lord*, as the One who has, or wants to have, all authority over their lives! "[I]n your hearts honor Christ as Lord . . ." (1 Pet. 3:15).

Jesus spoke about his commands several times, especially to his disciples during the last night of his earthly life: "A new commandment I give to you, that you love one another: just as I have loved you, you also are to love one another. By this all people will know that you are my disciples, if you have love for one another" (John 13:34-35). This is the basic Constitution of the Kingdom, the "royal (or, kingly) law," that is, the law of the King: "Love your neighbor as yourself" (James 2:8; cf. Lev. 19:18).

"If you love me, you will keep my commandments. . . . Whoever has my commandments and keeps them, he it is who loves me. And he who loves me will be loved by my Father, and I will love him and manifest myself to him. . . . If anyone loves me, he will keep my word, and my Father will love him, and we will come to him and make our home with him" (John 14:15, 21, 23). Jesus not only said, "Love your neighbor," but "Love *me.*" That is just as vital for the Kingdom of God: love for the King.

"If you keep my commandments, you will abide in my love, just as I have kept my Father's commandments and abide in his love. . . . This is my commandment, that you love one another as I have loved you. Greater love has no one than this, that someone lay down his life for his friends. You are my friends if you do what I command you. . . . These things I command you, so that you will love one another" (John 15:10, 12-14, 17). That is, "friendship" (intimacy with Christ) is joined to "commands" (obedience to Christ).

The Commands of God

The Christian gospel is not only about forgiveness and going to heaven—although these are important matters—it is about discipleship, it is about following Jesus in a world that rejected him. It is about accepting him, not only as your Savior, but as your Lord. The two are inseparable. You cannot accept him as Savior, in order to get to heaven, and at the same time refuse to accept and follow and obey him as Lord on this earth. "[I]f you confess with your mouth that *Jesus is Lord* and believe in your heart that God raised him from the dead, you will be saved" (Rom. 10:9, italics added). You not only follow him, but the true disciple wants to become *like* him: "It is enough for the disciple to be like his teacher" (Matt. 10:25).

This was even God's plan for you from eternity: "For those whom he [God] foreknew he also predestined to be conformed to the image of his Son" (Rom. 8:29). God "chose us in him [i.e., Christ] before the foundation of the world, that we should be holy and blameless before him"—like Christ (Eph. 1:4). "We all, with unveiled face beholding as in a mirror [or, reflecting] the glory of the Lord, are transformed into the same image from glory to glory, even as from the Lord the Spirit" (2 Cor. 3:18 ASV).

Christianity is not so much about waiting to go to Paradise when you die (cf. Luke 23:43), but about waiting for "our blessed hope, the appearing of the glory of our great God and Savior Jesus Christ" (Titus 2:13). Please remember: the saints in Paradise, and Jesus himself, at the right hand of God in glory, have not yet reached their final destination! On the contrary, they are all *waiting* for the same thing *we* are waiting for: Jesus is "waiting from that time [of his ascension] until his enemies should be made a footstool for his feet" (Heb. 10:13). In that age to come, believers will reign with Christ (1 Cor. 6:2; Rev. 5:10; 20:4, 6). But in the present age, believers are *subjects* of Christ in his Kingdom. And as such it is of the highest importance for them to know the rules of that Kingdom.

As subjects, Christians must—and are happily prepared to—

submit themselves to the commands of Christ. Actually we find only one single explicit command of Jesus: "Love one another," quoted above. But the fact that he spoke in the plural—"my commands"—indicates that there are many more commands of Jesus, of which the Love Commandment is the very kernel and highest note. The apostle Paul points out, "Keeping God's commands is what counts" (1 Cor. 7:19 NIV). In the book of Revelation, God's people are described as those "who keep the commandments of God" (12:17; 14:12). Those who, with a regenerated and loving heart, in the power of the Holy Spirit, do "the will of my Father who is in heaven" are those that "will enter the Kingdom of heaven" (Matt. 7:21).

Made Righteous to Produce Righteousness

This matter touches the heart of the Reformation. We are justified (made righteous) by faith alone. What an exquisite discovery! But what some children of the Reformation sometimes seem to forget is that a faith that does not result in lovingly keeping the rules of the Kingdom of God *is no true faith at all* (cf. Rom. 2:13; Gal. 5:6; James 2:14-26). Or in the words of Jesus, "Therefore whoever relaxes one of the least of these commandments and teaches others to do the same will be called least in the kingdom of heaven, but whoever does them and teaches them will be called great in the kingdom of heaven. For I tell you, unless your righteousness exceeds that of the scribes and Pharisees, you will never enter the kingdom of heaven" (Matt. 5:19-20). In other words, you have been justified (made righteous) by faith in order to *show forth* this righteousness. (In this connection, the suffix "-fication" in *justification* and *sanctification* comes from the Latin *facere*, "to make"; this is reflected in the Dutch words *rechtvaardigmaking* and *heiligmaking*, both of which include the idea of "making" righteous or holy, respectively.)

Conversely, if there is not this practical righteousness in a Christian's life, you may seriously wonder whether that person was truly justified (made righteous) by faith in the first place. The New Testament Epistles are full of this practical righteousness that is the fruit of the new life in the believer: "[P]resent yourselves to God as those who have been brought from death to life, and your members to God as instruments for righteousness" (Rom. 6:13; cf. vv. 16-18); "now present your members as slaves to righteousness leading to sanctification" (v. 19); ". . . filled with the fruit of righteousness that comes through Jesus Christ" (Phil. 1:11; cf. James 3:18). "Pursue righteousness, godliness, faith, love, steadfastness, gentleness" (1 Tim. 6:11; cf. 2 Tim. 2:22). In summary, the Kingdom of God is a realm of (very practical) "righteousness and peace and joy in the Holy Spirit" (Rom. 14:17).

Now, do you seriously think that God's commands are only those that are explicitly mentioned in the Scriptures? I definitely believe they also comprise his commands laid down in his creation—the commands that people sometimes call "creational ordinances." They cannot be read as easily as God's ordinances in Scripture; you have to put more effort into attaining knowledge of them. But that does not alter the fact that, for a disciple of Jesus, these commands as contained in creation are just as vital as any of the written commands. We know God, *and his commands*, through both nature and Scripture (cf. Belgic Confession, Art. 2).

In my book, *Wisdom For Thinkers*, (p. 76), I used the example of Isaiah 28:24-26. In this passage we see that it is God who instructs the farmer as to how he has to work his land, but in practice the farmer learns this by paying attention to the natural laws—which are *divine* laws—manifesting themselves in every crop. The farmer learns from the Lawgiver, not by literal words that the latter speaks, nor by reading the Bible, but by giving heed to his law-order, laid down in creation. This is the way the disciples of Jesus also learn from God, throughout the ages. The laws that are to be obeyed by his disciples are not necessarily explicitly found in Scripture—they may also be found in God's creation, if we only study it carefully. "Whoever *has* my commands and keeps them . . .," says Jesus (John 14:21, italics added). You must first *have* them before you can keep them. Sometimes they are easy to be "had," at other times they require a certain amount of study.

"Does not nature itself teach you . . .?" (1 Cor. 11:14). Applied to the matter of a Christian view of the state, this means that such a Christian view cannot simply be derived from a select number of Bible verses. That would be biblicism, which often also implies that the verses quoted are forced into some pre-conceived ideas about what the state is to be. No, if you want to understand what the state is, or what it is to be, *learn from the very nature of the state itself.* That is, analyze the phenomenon of the state, as well as the many forms the state has had throughout history, and do this in the light of a coherent Christian-philosophical view of cosmic reality (see again my *Wisdom For Thinkers*). Only in this way, you may get an idea of the divine creational ordinance concerning the state.

Criticism

Let us look at this problem of biblicism a little more closely. Sometimes, the doctrine of the Christian state as I have presented it so far, or similar forms of it, has been criticized for starting from a philosophical doctrine, and not simply from Scripture. If we would do the latter, it is argued, then the emphasis would be placed much less on some worldview, or some view of society, or some doctrine of the state, and much more on renewal of the heart, the inner experience of salvation. From there, the inner renewal would in the most natural way lead to a renewal of society, including political life.

Sometimes this criticism is phrased in the following way: neo-Calvinists build their state view on creation, whereas classical Calvinists and Evangelicals build their state view on re-creation, and on the "culmination of the ages." Neo-Calvinists look back (at creation), whereas classical Calvinists and Evangelicals look forward (to re-creation). Such critical objections are very important for a study concerning the state and the Kingdom of God! They deserve close attention. Let me therefore follow them one by one.

In the first place, we ought not to make a simplistic contrast between philosophy and Scripture. How do you think you could base a well-developed doctrine of the state directly on Bible verses? As I have repeatedly explained, the Bible does not contain doctrines and theories. You cannot possibly draw a full-fledged politicology, or political science, from the Bible because the Bible does not contain one. Designing a Christian political science is hard work, and there is no way you can avoid such a science being based upon a Christian-philosophical view of reality and knowledge.

Secondly, the renewal of the heart does not at all automatically lead to a renewal of political life. This will occur only *if you have a clear-headed idea as to what a Christian renewal of political life should look like.* Nowhere in history has a renewal of the heart as such ever led to a renewal of political life unless Christian thinkers developed certain models as to what a Christian state should look like. Where they failed to do this, even though their hearts were renewed, Christian thinkers simply assumed the pagan or semi-Christian state ideas around them; these ideas were Christianized a little, but they were not re-formed.

Thirdly, the contrast between a theoretical approach and an approach that begins with the renewed heart is a false one. It is nothing but a variety of the old contrast between structure and direction, a confusion that has plagued Christian thinking for such a long time. The doctrine of creation and creational ordinances, the doctrine of the state, etc., all involve the *horizontal* structure of cosmic reality. The matter of the renewed heart and the inner experience of salvation involve the *vertical* direction of human existence. These two dimensions cannot be played off against each other. Christian thinking should place as much emphasis on creational ordinances (horizontal), on the one hand, as on the inner life of the regenerated soul (vertical), on the other.

Fourthly, no Christian builds his doctrine of the state either on the notion of creation, or on the notion of re-creation alone. The two cannot be contrasted because they form a whole. Where people try to separate the two, we soon discover that such people are still caught in the age-old scholastic Nature–Grace dualism, which is the very thing we are trying to combat! Traditional (i.e., scholastic) Roman Catholic and Protestant thinking has suffered enough under the scholastic splitting of creation and redemption, of earth and heaven, of body and soul, of state and church, of general and special revelation, of the realm of God's power and the realm of God's grace, of providence and predestination, etc.

People who fall into this snare usually put off the radicality of God's Kingdom until the future of Christ's second coming and the establishment of the Messianic Kingdom, and limit the Kingdom of God in the present time to the inner pious life of the soul, or to the (invisible) church. What is left for everyday social and political life is at best, God's general goodness (cf. Matt. 5:45; Acts 14:17), which maintains the creational ordinances as well. Of course, the latter are thought to help advance God's salvation, but they themselves supposedly do not belong to this plan of salvation. In this way, the cleft between (the original) creation and re-creation (as part of the plan of salvation) is regrettably maintained.

Elevation

Radical Christian thinking has fundamentally broken with all these false contrasts and dualisms. It is firmly based on both the biblical notion of creation and the biblical notion of re-creation. These two can never be considered apart from each other because, as I said before, it is the re-creation (renewal, restoration, elevation) of *this* creation that God has in mind. *Creation* is going to be delivered (Rom. 8:18-22), but *we* are not going to be delivered from creation. It is impossible to separate creation and the Kingdom of God because this is what the Kingdom of God is all about: the elevation of *this* creation by Jesus Christ, through the Holy Spirit, for the glory of God the Father. It will be a *new* world, but not in the sense of a replacement but of a renewal of *this* creation.

This does not imply a circular restoration, so to speak, as if in the end, at the "culmination of the ages," we will be back at Genesis 1, and as if everything could start all over again. That would almost be an affront to God: it takes Man five minutes to ruin God's creation, and it takes God thousands of years to restore everything to its original state. No, that is why I used the word *elevation*; it will be a "spiral" restoration: in the end we will be back at Paradise, but on an infinitely higher level than in the beginning. We will enjoy not an "other" creation, but the elevation of *this* creation. In his *Enchiridion*, the great church father, Augustine, spoke of *felix culpa*, the "fortunate fall": "God judged it better to bring good out of evil than not to permit any evil to exist." His teacher, Ambrose, also spoke of the "fortunate ruin" of Adam in the Garden of Eden, in that his sin brought more good to humanity than if he had stayed perfectly innocent. The elevation of God's creation occurs through fall and redemption. But it will still be *this* creation. Therefore, the creational ordinances remain most highly relevant.

As an example of how we can go astray, I quote Oepke Noordmans, one of the best known Dutch theologians of the twentieth century. He claims that only Genesis 1 and 2 speak about creation, and the rest of the Bible speaks about re-creation. Other Reformed theologians have rejected such a formulation, and I believe rightly so. The *whole* Bible is about *this* creation, about *its* redemption and renewal in and through Jesus Christ. Such a statement seems to indicate how much Noordmans' thinking—and that of many theologians in his wake—still presupposes the scholastic Nature–Grace dualism. I repeat: re-creation always concerns the redemption and renewal of *this* creation.

Conversely, although we focus on *this* creation, this does not mean that we view it only in its present form, as being "in the pains of childbirth" as a consequence of the fall. No, we learn to view it from the perspective of the re-creation, that is, of the Kingdom of God. In unmasking scholastic dualism, we will no longer separate creation and re-creation, or even place them in juxtaposition. On the contrary, they are retained in one single redemptive perspective, in which creation can no longer be isolated from re-creation, as though we are still in Genesis 1, and re-creation can no longer be isolated from creation, as though the creational ordinances have no significance anymore.

What a grace would it be if Bible-believing Christians would preach not only the gospel of God's grace for poor sinners, but also the gospel of the Kingdom, as the Lord asked us to do. Is our only message the gospel for the salvation of souls, without any contribution for the *totality* of Christian life? What is the Evangelicals' contribution to science, to the arts, to culture, to society, to politics? Today there are countries in Africa where, through intensive missionary work, the majority of souls have been won for Christ, at least outwardly. But already now we see the looming prospect that, if the gospel affects only souls, and not culture, society, politics, then within a few generations many of these souls will turn to Islam. This happens because it is *not* true that the salvational renewal of the souls automatically affects and renews society.

I am thankful for the Evangelicals' emphasis on redemption, on the world to come, on their zeal for gospel preaching, for their emphasis on the work of the Holy Spirit, on the renewal of spiritual life of individuals and families. I am also thankful for any Reformed emphasis on *this* creation, on creational ordinances, on the work of God's Spirit in culture, society, and politics. Perhaps sometimes there is too much Reformed emphasis on structure, and too much Evangelical emphasis on direction. In this respect, the two could wonderfully learn from each other and complete one another.

The Structure of the State

I repeat, one of the many creational ordinances that God has posited in creation concerns the state. Such an ordinance is always a principle, that is, a constant, timeless *principium* (literally, "beginning"), a starting point for the realization of this principle in a certain time and a certain cultural historical context. A creational principle always maintains its urgent appeal to us, even if the practical realization of it changes all the time. *Conservatism* is the political view that clings to a certain time-bound form of the state because it confuses this specific form with the underlying timeless creational principle. *Progressivism* strives for changes in an existing form of the state, but without giving heed to this underlying normative and constant structural principle for the state.

If we believe that the state is a creational given, this simply follows from the biblical testimony that there are governing authorities and common citizens, that all governing authority has been established by God, and that the authorities are "God's servants" (Rom. 13:1-7). But simply referring to such a passage is not enough. In Paul's time, Rome had a cruel and oppressive emperor, and this was certainly not what God had in mind for the people. Therefore, in Romans 13 Paul is *not* necessarily approving the way in which the constant (i.e., creational) principle of the state had been concretely realized in the Roman empire of his time. Rather, using my terms, Paul is referring to the underlying timeless principle of the state as God had originally given it. A state is a state, and as such has to be obeyed, even if it is a wicked realization of the good principle God had established. In other words, we will not read Romans 13 correctly if we do not consciously distinguish between the *principle* of the state and its practical *realization* of that principle. The former is always good because it was given by God; the latter may be very bad.

If the state is indeed an institution of God, this means that its basic structure has not been designed or invented by Man. The same holds for the other institutional relationships: marriage, the family, and the church. The normative structure of the state, this divine blueprint for the state, is anchored in the creational order, it is pre-given, Man cannot change it. But what he *can* change is the practical realization of this blueprint. There are even many ways this blueprint can be instantiated or realized. It is like the blueprint of a house: you can build that house in many different sizes, with many different building materials and colors, in many different environments; you can even deviate from the blueprint in many details; but the blueprint as such always remains the same.

In my book *Wisdom For Thinkers,* (see chapter 4), I explained the difference between the law side and the subject side of reality. God's normative blueprint for the state is the state according to its law side; that is why I spoke of a principle, a structural law. The concrete realizations of this blueprint, as brought about by Man at a certain time and place, is the state according to its factual side or subject side. The normative state structure, that is the state according to its law side, is constant, unchangeable. But the realized forms of the state, that is, the state according to its subject side, are very changeable. This diversity is due to the God-given freedom of Man. According to his "response-ability," Man gives a response to God's pre-given state principle in some way or another. Sometimes, Man does this in an expert way, namely, when the form of the state remains close to God's ideal as expressed in the normative principle. Sometimes, Man does it in a very bad way, so that the state is nothing more than a caricature of God's blueprint.

The most ideal way to practically realize God's blueprint is seen in the Kingdom of God. Here again we see the inner connection between creation and re-creation: the form of the state as it is realized in the Kingdom of God is based on the normative state principle as originally given in creation. In the Kingdom of

God, there is a highest authority, there are subjects, there are laws given by the King that are to be obeyed by his subjects. Out of pure love, the King seeks the best for his subjects, and out of pure love his subjects are keen to serve him. The state *principle* is the same for all states, good or bad; the state *form* is that of a perfect absolute monarchy.

State Subjectivism

If people have forgotten about the normative state principle as pre-given by God, if they have no idea anymore of the law side of reality, they invariably try to find the norm for the state on the subject side. This is what we may call *state subjectivism*. Basically, there are only two forms of this subjectivism: *individualism*—the individual is the starting point for this state form—and *collectivism*, in which one societal relationship (the state as such, or the church, or "the people") becomes the starting point for establishing the state.

Individualism originated in the late Middle Ages, together with so-called nominalism (the doctrine that universal principles exist only in the human mind), and became the starting point for classical liberalism (including today's libertarianism) in all its various forms. In this view, only the individual is accepted as true reality; every societal relationship is considered to be nothing more than the pure sum of individuals. No pre-given, normative blueprint for any societal relationship is accepted. Man realizes the state according to his own free, autonomous choices. Here "autonomous" means that Man's choices lie anchored in the independent individual, and not, for instance, in some creational order that lies outside the individual and appeals to him with divine authority. In this view, it is actually no longer the president or prime minister who has the highest authority, but the individual, who is responsible to nothing and no one except to himself. Insofar as the individual must give account to authorities and judges, he can accept this because it is individuals ("voters") who voluntarily have put these authorities and judges in place, and they remain at their posts as long as it pleases the voters. Behind this lies the idea of people's sovereignty, discussed in chapter 4.

The second possible alternative for a doctrine of creational ordinances is, as I said, *collectivism*. This approach starts not from any pre-given, normative structures (on the law side), nor from the individual, but from certain concrete *collective* communities in reality (on the subject side), which are then absolutized. One of these communities is placed above the other ones. The best known examples of such absolutized communities are the following. (a) The state itself; in antiquity this was advocated by philosophers Plato and Aristotle, in modern times by socialists or social-democrats. (b) The church, as it is conceived in traditional Roman Catholic doctrine of the state; the result is the church state. (c) The people (German: *das Volk*), as it was conceived in German national-socialism; the result is the people's state. (d) The "world proletariat," when one day it will have triumphed in the "class struggle," which, interestingly, at the same time will imply the end of the state as such (Marxism). All other communities—families, schools, associations, etc.—are considered to be secondary, "organic parts" of the state, or the church state, or the people's state, or the communist state.

In both individualism and collectivism, the unique, irreducible nature of every societal relationship is lost altogether. Individualism basically denies this nature, socialism (and the traditional Roman Catholic doctrine of the state) subjects these communities to the state (in traditional Roman Catholicism: the church state). In both individualism and collectivism, the idea of the state is sought not outside Man, in a pre-given, normative creational order, that is, *in God*, but in Man himself. This characterizes not only individualism (see above), but also collectivism, because the doctrines of the state articulated in antiquity and the Middle Ages, grounded the state in human reason. Of course, in humanistic state doctrines this anchoring of the state in Man himself is even more obvious.

All these doctrines of the state, no matter how different they are, have this one thing in common: they deny creational ordinances, that is, they deny God's law. Subjective Man replaces God as Creator and Lawgiver. For Christians, I can see only these three options: (a) accept the divine law order, and therefore creational ordinances, or (b) fall into the snare of biblicism (i.e., building some kind of a state on the basis of disparate Bible verses—which usually produces nothing but some secular idea of the state), or (c) fall into the snare of secularism, that is, grounding the state, not in God's law, but in Man.

Questions for Review

1. What are some implications of "the gospel of the Kingdom" for the church's mission message?

2. Based on this chapter, explain what it means to teach those who are baptized everything Jesus has commanded.

3. Why are justification and sanctification inseparable?

4. Why is our study of history, and science, and creation important for knowing God's commands?

5. What are three objections that some raise against grounding a Christian view of the state in a philosophy of creation rather than in Scripture?

6. What are four responses to these objections you identified for Question 5?

7. Why must creation and re-creation be kept together, for the sake of Christian political theory?

8. Why is it important to distinguish between the normative structure of the state and the historical realization(s) of that structure?

9. What historical forms of the state have arisen from either individualism or collectivism? Why are both of these "-isms" mistaken?

CHAPTER EIGHT

EN ROUTE TO THE KINGDOM

It has often been asserted that the Christian idea of the state presupposes sin. If there had been no fall into sin, no state would have been needed, it is claimed. Therefore, the state in its most elementary form is mentioned for the first time after the flood of Noah (Gen. 9; but then, why not directly after the fall in Gen. 3?). The Belgic Confession seems to embrace the same idea in Article 36: "We believe that *because of the depravity of the human race* our good God has ordained kings, princes, and civil officers. He wants the world to be governed by laws and policies so that human *lawlessness* may be restrained and that everything may be conducted in good order among human beings" (italics added). This does not necessarily exclude the idea of the state as a creational ordinance, yet the formulation is certainly striking.

By the way, the Westminster Confession, Chapter 23.1, has a much more positive approach to the function of the state: "God, the supreme Lord and King of all the world, hath ordained civil magistrates, to be, under him, over the people, for his own glory, and the public good: and, to this end, has armed them with the power of the sword, for the defense and encouragement of them that are good, and for the punishment of evildoers."

Various Foundations

Those holding the view that the state exists basically to restrain evil point to Romans 13, especially v. 4b: "If you do wrong, be afraid, for he does not bear the sword in vain. For he is the servant of God, an avenger who carries out God's wrath on the wrongdoer." However, the passage as a whole makes clear that the state is much more than that: the authorities commend those who do right (v. 3), they are God's servants for the good of the people (v.

4a), they collect taxes (vv. 6-7), with which they do much more than just restrain evil. We find both sides in 1 Pet. 2:14, ". . . governors as sent by him [i.e., the Lord] to punish those who do evil and to praise those who do good."

With the well-known triad *creation—fall—redemption*, we find three possible explanations for a concept of the foundation of the state:

(a) *Creation*. This is the point of view I defend in this book. The state is grounded in a creational ordinance. Direct biblical evidence for this is Genesis 1:26-28, where God says first, "Let us make mankind in our image, in our likeness, so that they may *rule* over the fish in the sea and the birds in the sky, over the livestock and all the wild animals, and over all the creatures that move along the ground" (NIV). After he created Adam and Eve, he said to them, "Be fruitful and increase in number; fill the earth and subdue it. *Rule* over the fish in the sea and the birds in the sky and over every living creature that moves on the ground" (NIV; italics added). This can only mean that, right from the outset, Adam and Eve were called to be king and queen of creation.

(b) *Fall*. This is the idea that the state presupposes the fall; in other words, that the state has been instituted to restrain evil (see above, the example of the Belgic Confession). We might argue that the notion of "sword power" in Romans 13 supports this view. I would rather say that the power of the sword has been *added* to the mandate of the state after the fall, and because of the fall. This does not change the fact that earthly government as such was already implied in Genesis 1.

(c) *Redemption*. The traditional Roman Catholic doctrine of the state has in fact grounded its conception of the state on the redemption motif. The redeeming grace of God in Christ is viewed as embodied in the church, which is considered to be the dominating societal relationship. This view presupposes the Nature–Grace dualism. From the "upper story" of grace, so to speak, the story to which the church belongs, the light of God's grace shines to the "lower story" of nature, to which the state belongs. The dualistically separated creation and re-creation notions now become motifs that are supposed to stand in a dialectical interaction throughout world history.

Creational Order and the Fall

By now it should be clear that we opt for possibility (a), namely, creation, but in close coherence with the notions of fall and re-creation. The fall had a direct effect upon the state insofar as it is viewed from the subject side: many false forms of the state originated from Man's sinful heart, including the state's arbitrariness, malfeasance, violence, oppression, terror, nepotism, neglecting the weak, etc. This is about what false states have been doing; as far as the subjects are concerned, there has been disobedience, rebellion, anarchy, revolution, reactionism, etc. In a sense, the fall had an effect even on the state's law side: as I mentioned above, to the state as a creational ordinance was added the power of the sword to restrain evil.

In order to better understand the distinction between the law side and the subject side of the state, let us look at the effect of sin on the state as it is described in Romans 13 and in Revelation 13. In the former passage, written in the time of the cruel, terrorizing emperor Nero, the apostle Paul presents the state in an ideal form, according to its law side. He does not view it according to its subject side, that is, as the empire to which Nero and his predecessors had actually given form. However, in Revelation 13 we see basically the same Roman empire (though in an eschatological context) as a state viewed from the subject side, in its most anti-normative form: blasphemy instead of servitude, an outright cult of Satan, malfeasance, violence, oppression of God's people, hatred toward God himself.

After the fall into sin, God has maintained his creational order. In my book, *Wisdom For Thinkers*, (see p. 78), I tried to explain that sin could never change God's law order as such, because that order is nothing but the Word of his own mouth. Sin does not, and cannot, affect the structures as such, but only the direction of the human heart, which functions in all these structures. Sin did not affect the state on the law side but only on the subject side. According to the law side, the state is still "normal" because its law structure has not changed. According to the subject side, the state has become "abnormal" as a consequence of sin (Johan A. Heyns). In other words, the radical antithesis between good and evil does not function on the law side but on the subject side of reality. Over against the God-oriented direction, we find the apostate direction. Both God-oriented and apostate families, churches, states, schools, companies, associations, etc. stand under the same divine law order, but they function out of different directions of the human hearts. Both in God-oriented and apostate states, the normative state structure always remains presupposed, even though the apostate state lives in disobedience as a parasite on God's law.

There can be no tension between God's creation before the fall and God's re-creation after the fall. The reason is that God's good creation before the fall aimed at full shalom, complete blessing and perfect bliss for humanity, in communion with God and for his glory. It was Man's calling to travel this route of *shalom*, that is, the route of the unfolding all of creation's potentialities, the route of God's command to work the earth and take care of it (Gen. 2:15; cf. 3:23). Before sin entered the world, *this* was the "way of life" (see for the expression Prov. 5:6; Jer. 21:8; 1 Cor. 4:17; 6:4, although these verses refer to the time after the fall). After sin had entered, this remained the same path of life, but traveled now in the power of the redemption in Christ, through the Holy Spirit.

God's One Creational/Re-Creational Word

This is the very reason why creation "in the beginning" and the Kingdom of God in the "culmination of the ages" can never be played off against each other. Of course, there are great differences between the world as it would have developed without a fall—if we can at all imagine such a world—and the world as it did in fact develop after the fall. But this gives us no reason to manufacture a *contrast* between God's creational Word and his redemptive Word. It is one Word of God. I refer again to Article 2 of the Belgic Confession, "We know him [i.e., God] by two means: first, by the creation, preservation and government of the universe; . . . . Second, he makes himself more clearly and fully known to us by his holy and divine Word as far as is necessary for us in this life, to his glory and our salvation." I do not object to this confession—which is not a theoretical exposition of the subject but a confession of practical faith—as long as this pre-theoretical confession is not translated into a theoretical scholastic scheme of two different revelations.

It is past high time that in Christian philosophy, Christian theology, and Christian political science the insight begins to function that *all things* were created by God in, through, and for Christ, that *all things* hold together (or consist) in Christ, and that all things are to be reconciled to God through Christ (Col. 1:16-17, 20). Three times in one passage the apostle Paul speaks of "all things," and in all three cases they apparently are the *very same things*! There is only one creation of God, one revelation of God, one providence of God, and one redemption of God.

God's creational Word was never replaced by some re-creational Word. Sin did not alter God's creational Word as such; what it did was this:

(a) The creational Word has become a double-edged sword, in that it not only points to the way of life but also implies judgment upon the apostate, that is, those who deviate from it in a spirit of rebellion.

(b) In its original purpose God's creational Word is still sufficient, but it no longer suffices for the misery caused by sin. Therefore, it is not replaced but extended, or rather, "reformulated" into God's re-creational or redemptive Word (in the lingual form of Scripture). Thus, it is and remains God's *one* Word in Christ, through whom he has created, and through whom he re-creates (Andree Troost).

Because of this absolute continuity of God's creational/re-creational Word, his creational ordinances fully retain their force. "For truly, I say to you, until heaven and earth pass away, not an iota, not a dot, will pass from the Law until all is accomplished" (Matt. 5:18). We have to do with "the living and abiding word of God. . . . the word of the Lord remains forever" (1 Pet. 1:23, 25; remember, for Jesus and the apostles the "Scriptures" were what we call the Old Testament!). Thus, God's law for the state has not perished. Even less could one claim that the "new man" has nothing to do anymore with the state, and other societal relationships, because they allegedly belong to the "old creation." On the contrary, the apostle Paul describes the "new man" as coming to practical manifestation within the good, old relationships and communities formed by God's creating word: not only church, but also marriage, family, work (Eph. 4:22–6:9; Col. 3:9–4:1). Today he might have added school, company, association, and political party in his very practical exhortations.

Here again, we might easily confuse structure and direction. The "new creation" is not a new structure or structural order replacing the old order, but it is a radical renewal of the direction of the human heart. As a consequence, Man lives within God's creational order in a totally new way, that is, not sin-directed but Christ-oriented.

Alternative Views

In my humble opinion, those who reject the doctrine of creational ordinances do not have any workable alternatives. Actually, I know of only two basic alternatives, which I believe must both be rejected:

The first alternative is the Kingdom of God as *creatio continua* ("continual creation"). This idea implies a continuous work of divine creation within human history, particularly with regard to societal relationships. This involves the humanistic idea that creation means "the Creator creating creators." That is, the social and historical actions of Man throughout history are identified with God's continual creational acts. Man is considered to be the creator and re-creator of historically determined society, including the state. Ostensibly this occurs under the alleged providential guidance of God, but in fact it is autonomous Man who is active. In other words, God is totally passive; he never intervenes to stop the political actions of Man.

Among other things, this view has led to a "revolutionary" or "liberation theology," in which governments are overthrown and state institutions are destroyed. Usually this happens with the approval of more or less liberal theologians. The idea is that God makes all things new through people who, as God's partners, improve their societal relationships. The guidelines for such changes are derived, not so much from Bible verses, but from alleged "general principles" of the "new creation" or the "Kingdom of God" in its eschatological sense—principles designed and formulated by Man himself. To this end, terms like "new creation" and "Kingdom of God" are taken in a humanistic sense, not derived from God's unchangeable creational order. In this way, God is made subservient to the autonomous strivings of Man toward the Kingdom of God, viewed as it pleases Man. There are no fixed creational ordinances anymore. On the contrary, God (re-)creates the world and establishes his Kingdom through autonomous human actions.

As far as the *creatio continua* idea still recognizes a salvational history, this is a largely secularized one, whether it is in (semi-) Marxist theology (inspired by Ernst Bloch), in black theology (James Cone), in feminist theology (Mary Daly), in liberation theology (Gustavo Gutiérrez), in the somewhat older theology of hope (Jürgen Moltmann), the theology of work (Marie-Dominique Chenu), the theology of sexuality (Hermann Ringeling), the theology of history as such (Wolfhart Pannenberg), and other "genitive theologies."

The second alternative is that of the Kingdom of God as *creatio nova* ("new creation"). This idea implies the mistaken idea that, as I explained before, God's new creation is not a restoration and elevation of the original creation but a "new" creation in the sense of a replacement of the previous one. Over against this, I hold that the new creation is neither a replacement of the old creation, nor a simple restoration in the sense of a return to Genesis 1, but an elevation of the present creation.

The comparison with the resurrection body may be helpful here. On the one hand, this body will be just as different from our old body as the new creation is different from the old creation. The resurrection body is not "natural" anymore but "spiritual" (1 Cor. 15:44) (which does not exclude true corporeality; cf. Matt. 28:9; Luke 24:36-43; John 20:27). Jesus could enter in spite of closed doors (John 20:19), and his post-resurrection encounters had the character of an "appearance" (Mark 16:9; Luke 24:34; John 21:1, 14; cf. Acts 1:3). Nevertheless, Paul emphasizes that it is *this* mortal body that is raised at the resurrection of the dead (Rom. 8:11). There is both continuity and discontinuity.

Similarly, it is *this* creation that is going to be renewed, no matter how much more glorious that restored creation will be. It is *this* creation that God is going to bring to full fruition, unfolding, and completion. God never gives up on his original creation. If he would annul it by replacing it, he would in fact abandon it to sin and Satan. In a certain sense, that would imply a triumph for Satan, as I explained before.

Perhaps I should add here a few words on 2 Peter 3:10, "But the day of the Lord will come like a thief, and then the heavens will pass away with a roar, and the heavenly bodies [or, the elements] will be burned up and dissolved, and the earth and the works that are done on it will be exposed (some manuscripts: will be burned up)." See also Revelation 20:11b, "From his presence earth and sky fled away, and no place was found for them," and 21:1, "Then I saw a new heaven and a new earth, for the first heaven and the first earth had passed away." These verses seem to suggest that the first heaven and earth fully *disappear;* "burned up," "dissolved," "fled away," and "passed away" is certainly strong language. Yet, although the dead body almost fully decays in the grave, earlier I quoted Paul who said that it is *this* "mortal body" that is going to be raised again. Likewise, the earth will be dissolved, but it is *this* earth that is going to be restored. Remember, "taking away the sin [not 'sins,' but the *power* of sin] of the world" (John 1:29) will create such a dramatic change that it will never be the "same" world anymore. The world as characterized by sin and Satan will fully "disappear" (burn up, dissolve, flee away, pass away): "the world is passing away along with its desires" (1 John 2:17). But, in my view, this does not at all change the basic continuity between the old and the new world. "[T]he creation *itself* will be set free from its bondage to corruption," says Paul (Rom. 8:21, italics added). Not: creation will be replaced, but it will be delivered.

God's Kingdom and History

There is one creation, one creational revelation of God in Christ, and the unity and fullness of this revelation unfolds in creation, redemption, and the culmination of the ages. Of course, this unity of creation and of revelation does not exclude the diversity of the history of this creation. The events of creation, fall, redemption in

Christ, the establishment of the Kingdom of God in his person, its unfolding towards the culmination of time, to the "God all in all"—all of these events imply history. Christ, so to speak, is the point of unity, from whom the whole diversity of world history goes forth, in whom all historical diversity is concentrated, and in whom history will find its fulfillment and completion. In its widest sense, faith recognizes in all history the realization of the Kingdom of God in Christ, as well as the counter-forces that are constantly trying to disrupt this.

I like the ambiguity in Matthew 11:12, "From the days of John the Baptist until now the Kingdom of heaven has suffered violence [or, has been coming violently], and the violent take it by force" (NKJV). There is a double violence here, in both parts of the sentence. What Jesus means is that, *either* the Kingdom comes in with the violence of the Holy Spirit, *or* the enemies of the Kingdom try to stop it with Satanic violence. Concomitantly, the "violent" ones are either the disciples of Jesus, who must use spiritual violence to get in (cf. Luke 13:24, "strive to enter"), *or* the enemies, who want to eradicate it. This suggests a battle going on, in which violence is used on both sides: the "violence" of the Spirit—the Kingdom is one of "power" (1 Cor. 4:20)—over against the violence of Satan.

This battle can end with a victory for only one of the parties involved. A victory for Christ, therefore, also involves judgment on his enemies. This is a point of the greatest importance in our answer to adherents of the *creatio continua* idea (see above). In whatever form this idea is presented, as soon as it is asserted that God realizes his Kingdom through Man, *and only through Man*, what room is left for any divine action *against* Man? What room is left for a judgment on God's behalf upon all of Man's anti-normative actions? If Man's actions are fully autonomous, he cannot ever trespass any creational laws of God. In this case, there *are* no anti-normative actions anymore, and thus there cannot be any judgment of God: no judgment seat, no damnation, no providential judgments, no final judgment. This is exactly what many modernist theologians would like us to believe.

In his *Reformational Theology*, American theologian Gordon J. Spykman has called such approaches "two-factor" theologies, that is, theologies that do speak of God's and Man's actions but reject the "third factor," God's Word or law, according to which God judges the actions of Man: "For we must all appear before the judgment seat of Christ, so that each one may receive what is due for what he has done in the body, whether good or evil" (2 Cor. 5:10). How could there ever be a verdict at any fair tribunal if there were no law according to which certain actions are judged to be good or bad?

Rigidity and Dynamics

One reason why the idea of creational ordinances and their realization in history has often been despised and neglected is because of the false impression that this doctrine implies a static, rigid, sterile immutability. This alleged rigidity is then dualistically placed over against the vibrant, dynamic versatility of history, which is ascribed to (autonomous) human action. This idea betrays not only ignorance, but also a lack of understanding for the fundamental, continuous dynamics embedded within the creational order itself, and which are to be unfolded by Man in historical development. There is room for a tremendous changeability and dynamics, as long as these occur in obedience to the pre-given, normative structures that lie embedded within the creational order.

These structures do not imply a tight yoke, which "autonomous" Man would love to throw off. On the contrary, it is *his* very acting in an anti-normative way—within the state or wherever— that leads to decline, degeneration, and destruction. Creational ordinances were given by God not to make our Kingdom work dismal and burdensome, but to enable this very work in an optimal way.

This doctrine of creational ordinances should not be confused with that of traditional natural theology, which has done a lot of damage. Usually, this scholastic theology did not at all start with pre-given, normative structures embedded within the creational order (on the law side). Instead, it posited concrete, existing societal relationships (on the subject side). When people objected to these existing relationships, time and again this natural theology made the mistake of justifying the existing structures by frenetically clinging to the *status quo* with a false appeal to creational ordinances, or to the Logos, or to some kind of "natural law," or to substantial structures, or whatever they were called. It was a complete confusion between the law side and the subject side. The worst examples of this have occurred in "German-Christian" national-socialism, and other extreme forms of racism and *apartheid* ideas, which at times have all been justified by certain theologians.

However, just as out of place as this defense of the *status quo* was, so too was the overreaction of modernist theology, which has severed social structures from whatever kind of creational ordinances. This theology has absolutized and secularized these structures, entirely according to the demands of humanistic thinking, which is founded in the apostate idea of human autonomy. The tragedy from this is great: here, people are striving for the realization of the Kingdom of God on earth in the very spirit of autonomous independence, which is basically rebellion, which the King is going to judge when he comes again. David says, but through him the Messiah, "Morning by morning I will destroy all the wicked in the land, cutting off all the evildoers from the city of the Lord" (Ps. 101:8). The full-scale humanistic secularization of social life, including political life, cannot be softened by theologians masking it with a term like the Kingdom of God. That is just self-deception.

No matter how hard it is to say, we have to remind one another of the fact that there will be "fighters for the Kingdom of God" to whom the King will say one day, "I never knew you; depart from me, you who practice lawlessness!" (Matt. 7:23 NKJV). That is exactly what it is: "lawlessness" (Greek: *anomia*); not just trespassing the law, but being "without law," that is, not recognizing any divine law above oneself except those laws that Man's own free will and reason can accept. The apostasy of these lawless people consists in their rejection of God's law, including the ordinances that he has instituted for societal relationships. These people often speak of God and his Kingdom, and they often do so with a passion that is admirable. But it is a "two-factor" speaking: it is about God and Man, but not about God's commandments.

Finally: The Christian School

At the end of this study, I remind the reader once again of my actual subject: the central significance of the Kingdom of God and our Christian view of the state. The Lord reigns! But also: The Lord is coming! These are the two convictions that should pervade the whole of our Christian politics, in terms of both principle and practice.

Let me illustrate this once more with an example. It concerns a hot topic in several countries that until recently could still have been called Christian countries. It is the subject of free Christian education. The Christian school is not just a pragmatic matter involving a kind of ghetto education in a world that, for Bible-believing Christians, is increasingly becoming a threat. On the contrary, it is a matter of principle that Christians, at home, in church, *and at school* acquaint and familiarize their children and youngsters with the Lord and his dominion. Later on as adults, they can make their own choices. But it is our responsibility as Christian parents and grandparents to show them the way of life while they are still young. This is the pathway many of us learned to travel when we were young. We show it to our youngsters, as we are trusting Proverbs 22:6, "Train up a child in the way he should go; even when he is old he will not depart from it."

Or as Asaph said,

> I will utter dark sayings from of old,
> things that we have heard and known, that
> our fathers have told us.
> We will not hide them from their children,
> but tell to the coming generation
> the glorious deeds of the Lord, and his
> might, and the wonders that he has done.
> He established a testimony in Jacob
> and appointed a law in Israel,
> which he commanded our fathers
> to teach to their children,
> that the next generation might know them,

the children yet unborn,
and arise and tell them to their children,
so that they should set their hope in God
and not forget the works of God,
but keep his commandments
(Ps. 78:2-7).

The essential point I mentioned was: familiarize them with the Lord and his dominion, his Kingdom. This dominion concerns not only the functioning of schools and universities as such, but especially the contents of the lessons.

We want our children to be taught geography by experts who confess that "the earth is the LORD's" (Ps. 24:1; 1 Cor. 10:26) and that Jesus is the King of this earth (Matt. 28:18).

We want our children to be taught history by experts who confess that history is essentially the progress of God's Kingdom—with all the struggles that go along with it—or the "bringing," and in the end the re-bringing, "of God's Firstborn into the world" (Heb. 1:6).

We want our children to be taught modern literature by experts who know not only aesthetic values but also the moral principles of God's Kingdom.

We want our children to be taught natural sciences by experts who have knowledge of God's creation and its re-creation within the Kingdom of God.

We want our children to be taught religion by "the mature," by "those who have their powers of discernment trained by constant practice to distinguish good from evil" (Heb. 5:14).

Let me repeat: we wholeheartedly reject the illusion of neutrality in any domain, but certainly when it comes to educating the immature, our young people. There is no such thing as neutral religious education because the teacher can never be neutral. And if he or she is supposed to at least try to give a neutral *presentation* of religion, or religions, there is no reason why a Christian teacher could not do this just as well as a humanist, a liberal, or an atheist teacher. It is a nasty form of discrimination to suggest that Christian teachers of religion are more prejudiced than humanist, agnostic, atheist, socialist, or liberal teachers of religion.

By the way, those who plead for this kind of neutral education are themselves never neutral thinkers. It is always necessarily humanist, agnostic, Darwinist, Marxist, atheist, socialist, liberal, or revolutionary people who try to convince us of this illusion. They do not seem to be afraid of humanist, agnostic, Darwinist, Marxist, atheist, socialist, liberal, or revolutionary influences upon the school children. They do seem to be afraid of Christian influences upon the children. This is what is going on in countries that were formerly considered to be Christian, but now are being secularized with great speed. It is not neutrality that our opponents in fact want—it is secularization, that is, pushing religion to the edge of society. It is not religion lessons per se, but the Christian school as such, that is a thorn in their side.

It is my prayer that Christians in all our Western countries may wake up. To this end, I have written this book on the state and the Kingdom of God. Ultimately, God's Kingdom will surely triumph. But that does not prevent us from experiencing defeats locally if Christians are not watchful, and if they are not equipped with Christian insights into the status of state and school. Fight the lie of neutrality, and follow the closing words of the old apostle Paul (2 Tim. 4:1-4, 7-8, 18, italics added):

> "I charge you in the presence of God and of Christ Jesus, who is to judge the living and the dead, and by his appearing and his kingdom: preach the word; be ready in season and out of season; reprove, rebuke, and exhort, with complete patience and teaching. For the time is coming when people will not endure sound teaching, but having itching ears they will accumulate for themselves teachers to suit their own passions, and will turn away from listening to the truth and wander off into myths [like the myth of neutrality, wjo]. . . . I have fought the good fight, I have finished the race, I have kept the faith. Henceforth there is laid up for me the crown of righteousness, which the Lord, the righteous judge, will award to me on that Day, and not only to me but also to all who have loved his appearing. . . . The Lord will rescue me from every evil deed and bring me safely into his heavenly *kingdom*. To him be the glory forever and ever. Amen."

Questions for Review

1. What insights for the foundation of the state do we obtain from the triad "creation—fall—redemption"?

2. Why would it be better to ground the origin of the state in creation, rather than in the fall or in redemption?

3. Why should we not separate God's creational Word from his re-creational Word?

4. What are two alternative views to the doctrine of creational ordinances, and why is each defective?

5. What is meant by "two-factor" theologies, and why are they inadequate?

6. Distinguish between the doctrine of creational ordinances and what is called "natural theology."

7. What is the purpose and goal of Christian education?

8. Give examples of how the lie of neutrality affects education and politics.

CHAPTER NINE

THE CHRISTIAN SCHOOL UNDER ATTACK

A number of points mentioned in this book so far can best be illustrated by a relevant case study. I have chosen a lawsuit in which the freedom of the Christian school is at stake, by virtue of the authorities (in this case, of a Canadian province) assuming to themselves tasks that do not properly belong to them. I found the materials about this case on the website (arpacanada.ca) of the Association for Reformed Political Action (ARPA), located in Canada, and on the websites of several news services, especially Mondaq. This case involves the Loyola High School in Montreal, a private Roman Catholic (Jesuit) institution, not publicly funded. The texts on the ARPA website were written by ARPA lawyer André Schutten; I freely use them here with his kind permission.

The Issue

The Québec Ministry of Education, Sports, and Leisure had written its own Ethics and Religious Culture (ERC) course. The apparent aim was and is a deliberate effort to replace existing Roman Catholic and Protestant programs of religious and moral instruction in Québec's public schools with non-denominational ethical instruction and the presentation of various religions in a manner intended to be "cultural" rather than "religious," and "neutral" rather than "partisan." Whereas previously, students were allowed to choose between Roman Catholic instruction, Protestant instruction or a non-confessional morality and ethics course, from 2005 to 2008, the Québec Government gradually moved to replace this system with the single, mandatory ERC course. The Québec Minister of Education has stated that the change was intended to "better reflect the increasingly pluralistic reality of Québec."

Under the applicable legislation, the ERC course is mandatory for all students in grades 1-11 in Québec (with the exception
of grade 9 students), regardless of whether they attend public or
private schools or are homeschooled. Parents are not given the
option of exempting their children from the course.

The Loyola School had asked for an exemption from the re-
quirement to teach this material from a "neutral" perspective.
They already had included this course material (and more!) in a
religion program based on their own Roman Catholic perspective or worldview instead of the "moral relativism" of the course,
which was considered to be "incompatible with Roman Catholic
beliefs." This request for exemption was made on behalf of Loyola
High School's entire community, and was supported by expert
opinions on the merits of its program as compared to the Québec
ERC curriculum. In fact, ARPA has reported on a social-scientific, academic study conducted by Cardus (a Christian think tank
dedicated to the renewal of North American social architecture)
that demonstrates that independent, parent-run schools produce
better citizens.

However, the Québec Ministry of Education refused to grant
the exemption, so Loyola took the case to court. Their argument
is that prohibiting the teaching of religion and ethics from a religiously informed or confessional perspective in a private Roman
Catholic school infringes upon the religious right of a Christian
institution to ensure the religious and moral education of their
students in accordance with their convictions.

The arguments by Loyola High School included the following:
" . . . We believe that the methodological 'neutrality' proposed by
the ethics and religious culture program is problematic in theory,
because it implies a moral relativism that contravenes the beliefs
of many people and religions, including Catholicism. The proposed 'neutrality' is also unrealistic and impossible to achieve
in practice. (To honestly identify one's position is a more 'objective' approach than adopting a neutrality that one cannot really
achieve.) Our approaches differ from the standpoint of ethics, in
particular, but the goal of teaching respect for all, regardless of
our individual beliefs or customs, is of crucial importance for us.
As we mentioned in our last letter, our ethical ideal is not simply

to 'tolerate' others but indeed to 'love' others, as our Christian faith teaches us."

The Appeal

The trial judge accepted that position, stating at one point that the Québec government's refusal to tolerate any confessional perspectives was verging on totalitarianism. However, this favorable ruling by the Québec Superior Court was appealed by the province to the Québec Court of Appeal.

On December 4, 2012, the Court of Appeal released a shocking decision, one that has direct implications for other forms of Christian education in Canada, and perhaps elsewhere. The decision required Loyola High School to teach the province's ERC course, and to teach it from a "secular" perspective. The decision of the Court of Appeal declared that, because Loyola's own World Religions course is Roman Catholic in orientation, it could not be considered *equivalent* to the ERC program, because the ERC course was specifically designed to be religiously "neutral." The Court ruled that it is reasonable for a government to require a Christian school to set aside its own Christian worldview for an hour a day in order to teach about other religions and about ethics.

With this ruling, the Court of Appeal chose to overrule the decision of the Québec Superior Court, which was based on extensive expert evidence. It did so in favor of the ambitions of the Québec government, which stated that its program was better suited for greater tolerance in society.

It was not the first time that such a decision was taken by Canadian judges. In February 2012, the Supreme Court of Canada had ruled against parents who wanted to pull their children out of the mandatory course in a publicly funded school. The Supreme Court ruled that the parents had not demonstrated that the course objectively harmed their religious freedom.

After the Appeal Court's disappointing decision, Loyola High School applied on February 1, 2013, to the Supreme Court of Canada, seeking permission to appeal. On June 13, 2013, the Supreme Court accepted the application, and the appeal will be heard in April 2014. All supporters of Christian education in Canada, and in other countries as well, should be very interested in the outcome of this case. Reformed Christian denominations, for example, run their own independent schools, and the Québec Court of Appeal decision would pose an astounding infringement on how Reformed Christians, in fact *all* Christians, raise their children in what they consider to be a biblical way.

ARPA Canada plans to intervene at the Supreme Court of Canada to advocate for the principle that governments must recognize the paramount role of parents in the education of their children, especially in subjects such as religion, ethics, morality, and sexuality. ARPA is of the opinion that the Supreme Court needs to protect the freedoms of religion and association from the totalitarian impulses of the provincial government of Québec, and to recognize and affirm the right and benefit of allowing the Christian worldview to compete in the public square.

Arguments by the Québec Minister of Education

Here are some of the arguments that the Québec Ministry of Education used in its reply to Loyola High School:

". . . According to the summary of the program proposed by Loyola High School and submitted to the department for evaluation, the program is based on the Catholic faith and its main goal is the transmission of Catholic beliefs and convictions. It encompasses a conception of others, but once again from a Christian Catholic perspective.

"Again according to the summary of the program submitted to the department for evaluation, it appears that, contrary to the Ethics and Religious Culture program, the Loyola High School program does not lead the student to reflect on the common good, or on ethical issues, but rather to adopt the Jesuit perspective of Christian service. . . .

"The training in religious culture of the Ethics and Religious Culture program is aimed at an enlightened comprehension of the many expressions of the religious experience present in Québec culture and in the world. Each religious tradition is observed individually without comparison or reference to another tradition. According to the summary of the program proposed by Loyola

High School and transmitted to the department for evaluation, the program does not meet the requirements for the Ethics and Religious Culture program in terms of religious culture, as religions are studied in connection with the Catholic religion.

"Again according to the summary of the program submitted to the department for evaluation, the program proposed by Loyola High School is distinguished from the Ethics and Religious Culture program in terms of the teacher's role. In the Ethics and Religious Culture program, the teacher's foremost responsibility is to assist and guide the students in their reflections, whereas according to the information provided the department, the teacher of the program proposed by Loyola High School seems to have to teach the foundations of the religion and universe of Jesuit Catholic beliefs."

Counter-Arguments

Note carefully what is going on in the Ministry's reasoning just quoted. The arguments of the Ministry are very simple. The Loyola program is at variance with the ERC program, the ERC program is to be implemented in every high school in Québec. Consequently, there is no place for the Loyola program. The underlying basic questions are not even addressed, much less answered.

First, the existence of the Ethics and Religious Culture program in itself is amazing enough. It is ludicrous that a country on the one hand permits the existence of schools with a religious background (Roman Catholic, Protestant, Jewish, Muslim, whatever), but on the other hand refuses to allow those schools the right to teach religion to their own pupils in their own way! It is like saying: We allow your religious school, but *we* will teach religion to your students, because we trust ourselves better in this respect than we trust you. But why then have religious schools in the first place, if these schools are not even allowed to handle their own core business? It very much looks like a first attempt to get rid of the Christian schools in Québec altogether.

Secondly, the more fundamental question is this: Is it the task of a state or province to teach ethics and religion? Not at all. Teaching religion goes way beyond the actual task of the state, which is to maintain public justice. It is a first characteristic of the totalitarian state, which arrogates to itself all kinds of tasks that actually belong to other societal relationships, in this case, the school. Of course, the state has to ensure the *quality level* of school programs, in order to protect the children against inferior education. Inferior education would not be in the state's best interest. But the state has nothing to do with stipulating the religious or ideological *orientation* of school programs. The state may not blame a Roman Catholic or a Protestant school for desiring to teach religion in a Roman Catholic or a Protestant way, respectively. Why else would a Roman Catholic or a Protestant school exist in the first place?

Thirdly, both the Québec Ministry of Education and the Court of Appeal apparently believe in the fairy tale of "neutral" education. I quote here the words by Dr. Douglas B. Farrow, professor of Christian thought at McGill University (Montreal), who testified as an expert witness during the trial of this case: ". . . first, that the Ethics and Religious Culture (ERC) program represents a significant transfer of power from civil society to the state; second, that its ambitious goals belie any claim to neutrality; third, that the ERC program is intended to provide formation (i.e., to cultivate a world view and a way of thinking and acting consistent with that world view) and not merely information, and that the formation it hopes to provide is at points incompatible with a Catholic formation; fourth, that the imposition of this curriculum (with its compulsory pedagogy) on Catholic schools constitutes, from the perspective of the Catholic Church, a breach of fundamental rights as well as a defeat for certain of the program's own objectives in recognizing diversity."

And elsewhere: "What is particularly insidious about the universal imposition of the ERC program is that it undermines all three constituent freedoms [i.e., freedom of religion, of thought, and of conscience, wjo]. It does so by purporting to defend the first of them, but in such a way as to seize from parents the primary responsibility for cultivating that freedom, and from the Catholic Church its educational mission. Against this stands the claim of *Dignitatis humanae* [a declaration on religious freedom by pope Paul VI, 1965, wjo] that parents 'have the right to determine, in accordance with their own religious beliefs, the kind of religious education that their children are to receive,' and that 'the rights of parents are violated if their children are forced to attend lessons or instructions which are not in agreement with their religious beliefs.' Against it stands also the claim that 'the Catholic school forms part of the saving mission of the Church, especially for education in the faith.' Against it stands indeed Canada's obligation as spelled out in articles 10 and 13 of the *International Covenant on Economic, Social and Cultural Rights* [of the United Nations, 1966. WJO], and the desire of Québec society to preserve and enhance liberty of thought, liberty of conscience, and liberty in religion."

Arguments by the Court of Appeal

The Court of Appeal ruled that the Ministry of Education's refusal to grant Loyola High School an exemption was a decision within the sphere of discretion conferred upon her by the legislature in designing and implementing the Course. Indeed, it was consistent with the legislative intent to "deconfessionalize" education in Québec.

The Minister's decision that the alternative course taught by Loyola High School was not equivalent to the ERC course was entitled to a high degree of deference from the Court. While the two courses were similar, Loyola's course was undoubtedly taught from a Roman Catholic perspective. The Minister was within her discretion when deciding that the objectives of the ERC course could not be fulfilled if taught from a religious perspective.

There was doubt as to whether Loyola High School, as a corporate body, was entitled to freedom of religion (a right possibly accorded only to individuals under the Canadian *Charter of Rights and Freedoms*). (The Québec Attorney General argued that, as a "moral person," in the sense of a corporation, organization, or institution, the school did not have the right to freedom of religion under the Canadian *Charter of Rights and Freedoms*. While the Court of Appeal skirted this issue, the Supreme Court of Canada will be presented with this question directly.)

The Court of Appeal also ruled that there was no significant infringement of religious rights in this case, given that the ERC course was only one of many courses taught at the school, and did not require teachers to refute Roman Catholic beliefs, but only to refrain from expressing their opinions or convictions about any of the religions discussed in the ERC course. Requiring Loyola High School to teach various religious beliefs from a global and ethical perspective without requiring adherence to those beliefs did not constitute an infringement of religious freedom. It simply entailed Loyola High School putting aside its Roman Catholic perspective for the duration of one class. Even if there were an infringement of religious freedom, that infringement was justified by the important course goals of acknowledging diversity and the pursuit of the common good.

Comments on the Appeal Court's Decision

First, the verdict of the Québec Court of Appeal itself is, of course, not a "neutral" one. It implies a defense of the secular state with the idea that the secular state is better equipped than Christian teachers to teach Christian children about religion. This idea is not based on social-scientific research but apparently only on the pre-conceived ideology of the secular state. One might say that, apparently, it is the ideology of the Québec Court of Appeal that Québec is to take a "neutral" stand toward all ideology except the ideology of the secular state as such.

Secondly, if the Court is of the opinion that the state's religious program is better suited for greater tolerance in society, the Court does not show this tolerance itself toward the Christian (Roman Catholic or Protestant) worldview. The Court of Appeal has seriously infringed upon the right of parents to direct the religious education of their own children. This precedent-setting decision creates a dilemma for Roman Catholic parents in Québec, and indeed for all Christian parents who may seek to send their children to a private or independent Christian school. Christians want to provide their children with an authentic moral and religious upbringing in accordance with their faith and religious worldview. This is a right that a robust understanding of the Canadian *Charter of Rights and Freedoms* should recognize and guarantee.

Thirdly, the teaching of world religions as preferred by the

Court of Appeal devalues religion in favor of a phenomenological and relativistic approach. The judgment gives more clout to provincial governments across the country, some of which devalue the religious rights of their citizens and their institutions. The precedent has now been set for a forced separation between education and faith, between mandatory secular indoctrination and Christian worldview training. The Supreme Court of Canada urgently needs to correct this. It needs to uphold parental rights in education, to protect freedom of religion and association from the totalitarian impulses of government, and to recognize and affirm the right and benefit of allowing the Christian worldview into the public square.

Fourthly, the underlying policy is astonishing, to say the least. In fact, the Court of Appeal sets a precedent whereby the government can compel any Christian school to set aside its religious beliefs and values in order to teach certain subjects. How could one imagine Christian teachers having to teach Christian children that the Islamic, Buddhist, or Wiccan worldviews are as acceptable as the Christian worldview? Or how could one imagine Christian teachers discussing ethics and moral issues, for instance, such as abortion or homosexuality, from a position that is "religiously neutral"?

The decision of the Québec Court of Appeal, as well as similar decisions in related cases, evidences a clear preference for a secular approach towards religious instruction. It also exhibits an increased judicial tendency to limit administrators' and parents' right to control the religious instruction that their children receive in school, in order to promote multiculturalism and dialogue between religious faiths.

It is of the utmost importance that Christians everywhere in the Western world realize these underlying tendencies. They can take a stand, I feel, only if they fulfill certain essential conditions:

(a) They must develop a clear-headed Christian view of the state, and in that context also of the Christian school, and of the proper coherence of all societal relationships and communities.

(b) They must unmask the tendency of secularization (in the sense of excluding religion from public life), and the underlying false interpretation of the separation of church and state, as if this were the same as the separation between religion and society.

(c) They must refute the falsehood of religious "neutrality," behind which various "-isms" are concealed: religious and ethical relativism, multiculturalism, and usually liberalism or socialism.

It is my prayer that the present book may contribute to this necessary growing awareness of vital Christian principles.

CONCISE BIBLIOGRAPHY

N.B. I did not include any articles or book chapters.

For more general works on Christian philosophy, see the bibliography in my book *Wisdom For Thinkers*.

Bartholomew, C., Chaplin, J. & Wolters, A. (eds.). 2002. *A Royal Priesthood: The Use of the Bible Ethically and Politically*. Grand Rapids: Zondervan.

Chaplin, J. 1985. *The Gospel and Politics: Five Positions*. Toronto: Institute for Christian Studies.

Clouser, R.A. 1991, 2005. *The Myth of Religious Neutrality: An Essay on the Hidden Role of Religious Beliefs*. Notre Dame: University of Notre Dame Press.

Dooyeweerd, H. 1968. *The Christian Idea of the State*. Nutley: The Craig Press.

Dooyeweerd, H. 1979, 2003 (repr.). *Roots of Western Culture: Pagan, Secular, and Christian Options*. Lewiston: Edwin Mellen Press.

Dooyeweerd, H. 1986. *A Christian Theory of Social Institutions*. Jordan Station: Paideia Press.

Dooyeweerd, H. 2008 (repr.). *The Struggle for a Christian Politics*. Lewiston: Edwin Mellen Press.

Fowler, S. 1985. *Biblical Studies in the Gospel and Society*. Potchefstroom: PU for CHE.

Fowler, S. 1988. *The State in the Light of the Scriptures*. Potchefstroom: PU for CHE.

Fowler, S. (ed.). 1990. *Christian Schooling: Education for Freedom*. Potchefstroom: PU for CHE.

Goudzwaard, B. 1972. *A Christian Political Option*. Toronto: Wedge.

Goudzwaard, B. 2001. *Globalization and the Kingdom of God*. Grand Rapids: Baker Books & the Center for Public Justice.

Groen van Prinsterer, G. (1847) 2000. *Unbelief and Revolution: A Series of Lectures in History*. Jordan Station: Wedge.

Hancock, R. 1989. *Calvin and the Foundations of Modern Politics*. Ithaca: Cornell University Press.

Heffernan Schindler, J. (ed.). 2008. *Christianity and Civil Society: Catholic and Neo-Calvinist Perspectives*. Lanham: Lexington Books.

Joireman, S.F. (ed.). 2009. *Church, State, and Citizen: Christian Approaches to Political Engagement*. New York: Oxford University Press.

Lugo, L.E. (ed.). 2000. *Religion, Pluralism, and Public Life: Abraham Kuyper's Legacy for the Twenty-First Century*. Grand Rapids: Eerdmans.

McCarthy, R.M., Oppewal, D., Peterson, W. & Spykman, G. 1981. *Society, State, and Schools: A Case for Structural and Confessional Pluralism*. Grand Rapids: Eerdmans.

McCarthy, R.M., Skillen, J.W. & Harper, W.A. 1982. *Disestablishment a Second Time: Genuine Pluralism for American Schools*. Grand Rapids: Eerdmans.

Marshall, P. 2002. *God and the Constitution: Christianity and American Politics*. Lanham: Rowman & Littlefield.

Monsma, S. & Soper, J.C. (eds.). 1998. *Equal Treatment of Religion in a Pluralistic Society*. Grand Rapids: Eerdmans.

Mouw, R. 1976. *Politics and the Biblical Drama*. Grand Rapids: Baker.

Mueller, W.A. 1965. *Church and State in Luther and Calvin*. Garden City: Doubleday Anchor Books.

Neuhaus, R.J. (ed.). 1987. *The Bible, Politics, and Democracy*. Grand Rapids: Eerdmans.

Ouweneel, W.J. 2014. *Wisdom For Thinkers: An Introduction to Christian Philosophy*. Jordan Station: Paideia Press.

Skillen, J.W. (ed.). 1982. *Confessing Christ and Doing Politics*. Washington: APJ Education Fund.

Skillen, J.W. 2004. *In Pursuit of Justice: Christian-Democratic Explorations*. Lanham: Rowman & Littlefield.

Skillen, J.W. & McCarthy, R.M. (eds.). 2001. *Political Order and the Plural Structure of Society*. Grand Rapids: Eerdmans.

Spykman, G.J. 1992. *Reformational Theology: A New Paradigm for Doing Dogmatics*. Grand Rapids: Eerdmans.

Storkey, A. 2005. *Jesus and Politics: Confronting the Powers*. Grand Rapids: Baker Academic.

Strauss, D.F.M. 1999. *Being Human in God's World*. Bloemfontein: Tekskor.

Taylor, E.L.H. 1966. *The Christian Philosophy of Law, Politics and the State*. Nutley: Craig Press.

Van Riessen, H. 1965. *Christian Approach to Politics*. Amsterdam: Vrije Universiteit.

Van Til, C. 1979. *Essays on Christian Education*. Phillipsburg: Presbyterian & Reformed Publishing.

Wolters, A. 1986. *Creation Regained: A Transforming View of the World*. Leicester: Inter-Varsity Press.

SCRIPTURE INDEX

John 14:21	94
John 14:30	3, 35
John 15:10, 12-14, 17	91, 93
John 15:18-20	69
John 13:16	69
John 16:11	3, 35
John 17:11	60
John 17:14-16	60
John 18:36	4
John 19:11	1
John 20:19	111
John 20:27	111
John 21:1, 14	111
Acts 1:3	111
Acts 1:8	2
Acts 3:31	3
Acts 4:19	40, 42
Acts 5:29	40, 42
Acts 14:17	97
Acts 14:22	69
Acts 15:14	52
Acts 20:28	41
Romans 1:20	60
Romans 2:13	93
Romans 3:19	60
Romans 4:11, 13	74
Romans 4:17	32
Romans 6:12	51
Romans 6:13, 16-18	93-94
Romans 6:19	94
Romans 8:11	111, 112
Romans 8:18-22	97
Romans 8:21	112
Romans 8:29	92
Romans 8:38-39	10
Romans 9:24-25	52
Romans 10:9	11, 92

SUBJECT INDEX

Absolutism, 102, 115
Ambrose, 97-98
Ancient Israel, 51-53
Aquinas, Thomas, 75. See also Scholasticism
Aristocracy, 46-47, 49-50
Aristotle, 102
ARPA, 121-122, 124. See also Loyola High School
Augustine, 83, 97
Authority, 3, 5, 8-9, 14-15, 21, 26-27, 37-43, 47-49, 55-57, 69, 71, 76, 78, 80-81, 90-91, 99, 101
Autonomy, 32-33, 38, 47, 56, 75, 84, 101, 110-111, 113-115

Belgic Confession
    Article 2, 94, 108
    Article 36, 55-57, 80, 105-106
Biblicism, 94-95, 102-103
Bloch, Ernst, 111

Calvin, John, 80, 82
Cardus, 122
Chenu, Marie-Dominique, 111
Christian politicology, 45-46, 52, 59, 95-96
Church (Body of Christ), 39-40, 52-53, 74
Church (Denominations), 2, 4, 6-8, 13-16, 19-28, 34-43, 53-57, 61-66, 69, 71, 73-85, 96-97, 100-102, 106, 108-110, 116, 129-130. See also Societal relationships
    Anabaptist, 62, 79
    Anglican (Church of England), 14, 27, 79-82
    Calvinist, 79, 95
    Evangelical, 89, 95, 98-99
    Full Gospel, 90
    Lutheran, 17, 27, 75, 78-79, 81-82
    Neo-Calvinist, 62, 95
    Orthodox, 27
    Protestant, 16, 56, 79, 96, 121, 125-126, 128
    Reformed, 13-14, 55-57, 62, 79-82, 90, 98-99, 124
    Roman Catholic, 6, 13, 15-16, 27, 34-35, 43-44, 62, 79, 81-82, 84-85, 96, 102, 106, 121-128

Re-creation, 77-78, 89, 95-98, 100-101, 106-111, 117
Reality
       Law-side, 63, 100-102, 107-108, 114-115
       Subject-side, 63, 100-102, 107-108, 114-115
Relativism, 122, 129-130
Religion, 6-7, 15-16, 18-20, 22, 24, 32, 44, 52, 54-56, 77-80, 85, 117-118, 121-130
Responsibility, 16, 31, 33, 43, 55, 64-67, 73, 82-83
Righteousness, 3-4, 16-20, 22, 25-28, 74, 89, 93-94
Ringeling, Hermann, 111

Scholasticism, 62, 74-75, 81-83, 96, 98, 108-109, 114. See also Nature-Grace dualism
Schools, 2, 4-8, 11, 13-16, 18-19, 22-27, 33, 35, 37-40, 42-43, 48-49, 54, 63, 65, 69, 76, 78, 84-85, 102, 108, 110, 116-118, 121-129. See also Societal relationships
Secularization, 7, 18, 74, 76, 85, 102-103, 111, 115, 118, 129-130
Sexuality, 21-22, 26, 124, 129
Sin, 3-4, 7, 19, 21, 32-33, 36-37, 42-43, 46, 51, 59-64, 68-70, 81, 86, 90, 97-98, 105, 107-110, 112
Societal relationships, 2, 5, 7-8, 15-16, 18-20, 25-28, 31-32, 34, 36-40, 48-49, 51, 53-54, 61-66, 68-69, 73, 76, 81-86, 89, 100-102, 106, 109-110, 114-115, 126, 129. See also Church, Companies, Family, Marriage, Political parties, Schools, State
Socialism, 14-15, 23-24, 33-34, 85, 102, 130
Society, 6-8, 16, 18, 24-25, 32, 35-37, 55, 59-62, 69-70, 78, 84, 89-90, 95, 98-99, 110, 118, 129-130
Sphere sovereignty, 6, 13-19, 57, 85. See also Kuyper, Abraham
Spykman, Gordon J., 113-114
State, 1-2, 4, 6-9, 11, 13-16, 18-27, 33-43, 46-49, 51-57, 63-65, 69, 71, 73-86, 89-90, 94-96, 99-103, 105-110, 114, 116, 118, 125-126, 128-130. See also Societal relationships
Strauss, Herman J., 26
Structure, 31-36, 46-47, 51-54, 60-64, 69, 82-86, 96, 99-100, 107-108, 110. See also Vollenhoven, Dirk
Subsidiarity, 84-85

Theocracy, 16-17, 45-48, 50-55, 82-83
Theology, 75-77, 80-81, 98, 109-111, 113-115
Totalitarianism, 44, 77, 123-124, 126, 129
Troost, Andre, 109
Two-kingdoms doctrine, 74-78, 81